D0089536

The History Plays

Also by David Hare

SLAG
TEETH 'N' SMILES
FANSHEN
A MAP OF THE WORLD

(with Howard Brenton) BRASSNECK *(Methuen)*

Films for television
DREAMS OF LEAVING
SAIGON: YEAR OF THE CAT

The History Plays

KNUCKLE   LICKING HITLER   PLENTY

David Hare

faber and faber
LONDON·BOSTON

This collection first published in 1984
by Faber and Faber Limited
3 Queen Square London WC1N 3AU
Filmset by Wilmaset Birkenhead
Printed in Great Britain by
Whitstable Litho Ltd Whitstable Kent
All rights reserved

British Library Cataloguing in Publication Data

Hare, David
The history plays.
I. Title
822'.914   PR6058. A678

ISBN 0–571–13132–8

Contents

Introduction

I started writing *Knuckle* in the same way I had written my previous two plays—on my lap. Running Portable Theatre in the late 1960s and early 1970s was a full-time job, and I used to snatch what time I could to write, never admitting to myself that I was becoming a playwright, choosing instead always to see myself as a theatre director who occasionally wrote.

My early plays, people told me, were satire, though I myself had no sense of it. Looking back, I can see that their view was probably correct. Beyond knowing that my own schooldays provided some background to the farce, I have to this day little idea where *Slag* came from, and I have no urge to find out, either by reading the play again or by being forced to sit through it. I set off writing *Knuckle* in a customarily careless and lazy way, inspired by the idea of expressing my love of thrillers on the stage. But the sudden loss of my manuscript in a dustbin in Amsterdam concentrated my mind.

My early manner of writing had been to start at the beginning, fill a certain number of pages and stop when the job was done. I travelled with a typewriter. One night I made the mistake of leaving the first thirty pages of *Knuckle* in the auditorium of the Mickery Theatre, where I was then working. By the morning they had been gathered up and thrown out by the eager Dutch cleaning ladies. A search of the huge metal cylinders at the back of the theatre revealed that the garbage trucks had already called. It is one of the oddest features of those days that all the most doped-out children of the West chose as their favourite meeting place one of Europe's most efficient bourgeois cities.

Having to start again did me a great deal of good. Since then, writing has never been so easy. It now takes me a year, or sometimes two, to write a play, but I am sure I benefited from Life telling me so clearly: Now Think This Time. I had conceived of a pastiche, and I suppose indeed a good deal of the dialogue of the final play still bears the marks of that decision. But indiscernibly, as I began to work again, a purpose emerged as well: to subvert the form of the thriller to a serious end.

In this I was only doing what many had done before me. I have no snobbery about thrillers. From childhood they have been the form of literature I have understood best, and my enthusiasm is indiscriminate. I still enjoy Dick Francis as much as John Dickson Carr, whose locked-room mysteries, you may say, represent the pure detective story at its most refined. If I have a preference at all, it is for those who work against the form to make it do something to which it is not apparently suited. In Patricia Highsmith's books there is no obvious mystery except the mystery of why we are alive. She works against the expectations of the genre to make violent action seem neither colourful nor dramatic but commonplace, fitting all too easily into ordinary lives. She banishes sentimental notions of guilt.

My purposes were cruder and less well ordered. Although I have been generally accused of predicting capitalism's final days a shade prematurely, I intended *Knuckle* in fact as an exhibition of capitalism's strengths and some guide to its intense emotional appeal. Capitalism adapts; and in the early seventies was adapting faster than usual to a change of mood in England. Underlying *Knuckle* is the feeling that there will no longer be any need for public life to be decked out in morality. In the last days of the Empire, English capitalism still dressed in a bespoke philosophy of service and intended civilization. But now politicians were ready to stand on a platform of bad-tempered self-interest, with only the most formal claims on the electorate's higher feelings. Out for Number One was suddenly to be the acceptable political creed of the day. In this, *Knuckle*, God help us, foreshadows the arrival of Mrs Thatcher, who likes to be thought of as a revolutionary, but whose true line of succession is from her hated opponent Edward Heath. The press loves to call her a crusader, but the title is decorative only, mere camp. A crusade for yourself is no crusade at all.

This my unlikeable hero Curly Delafield discovers but chooses to ignore, thereby losing the love of Jenny Wilbur, who was played in the original production by the young Kate Nelligan, of whom

Michael Codron had heard good things. She, Edward Fox, Michael Blakemore and I set off for our pre-London try-out with high expectations of success, although Edward, I think, had already begun to realize how inexperienced the writer was. Although the part of Curly is long, it has little variety. It is always going to be something of a chore to play a hero who, having made a discovery, chooses only to smother it. All too easily things turn into a one-note samba. I learned a great deal about loyalty and courage from Edward, for much as the students of Oxford loved us, the West End public did not. The wind used to sweep through the empty stalls as Edward, disturbed only by the sound of the loudest bartenders in London clattering their crates, would step forward to buttonhole a small and indifferent house with yet another monologue on the iniquities of capitalism. In this he never flinched. I admired him beyond words. One evening, I am told, the Comedy Theatre was almost empty but for the near-solitary figure of Colin Chapman, the inventor of Lotus Cars. For some reason that I cannot explain, this scene has always inflamed my imagination.

Edward's ordeal had been prolonged by the intervention of a man called Edward Sutro, a noted first-nighter who had rung Michael Codron the day after we opened to tell him that he wanted to be remembered as the man who had lost all his money on the original production of *Knuckle*. After four months of this behaviour he had to be forcibly restrained from more trips to the bank and gently told that the rest of us had decided to call it a day. I was sorry to see that his obituary in *The Times* made no mention of his wish.

My other great debt was to the inspiration Ross Macdonald's books had given me. I sent him a copy of the play, and he wrote a kind letter back, under his real name of Kenneth Millar. Most of the letter was about the threat to the seabirds of Santa Barbara, but he also said he had read my play and that although he was flattered that I had been influenced by him, he thought the play 'at a tangent' to his own work. I cannot imagine a more diplomatic phrase to use to a young writer who admires you.

I am able now to be relaxed about *Knuckle*'s commercial failure. It was, I believe, the only serious play to originate in the West End that year. All the others transferred from the subsidized sector. But at the time the hurt of its failure winded me very badly. I was aware for the first time that there was to be something about my plays which would attract the most impassioned opposition. In the days of Portable Theatre, when booed offstage by whole audiences, we would cheer ourselves up by insisting that the violence of the reaction was a measure of the success with which we had hit our intended targets. I wish I thought this explanation valid, but it smacks of false comfort. Apart from *Licking Hitler*, all of my plays have hit rough water as soon as they left the dock. In part I am sure this is because I at least write of subjects which are of true concern to the audience, and in a way which is deliberately impure. Pure ideas and ideals are deflected and strained through imperfect personalities which distort them. For some reason it seems to take both my audiences and my critics time to allow this process. Of course I wish it were otherwise.

Meanwhile I had begun to think about the war. I was born in 1947, and it makes me sad to think that mine may be the last generation to care about this extraordinary time in English history. Although I was thrilled by Angus Calder's proof in *The People's War* that it was the war itself which educated the working class towards the great Labour victory of 1945, I must also, if I am honest, admit that the urge to write about it came as much from a romantic feeling for the period: for its violence, its secrecy and, above all, its sexuality.

After I had finished *Plenty* and *Licking Hitler* I found something Alan Ross had written which catches this flavour as well as it can be caught: 'The sadness and sexuality and alcohol were what everyone was wanting, and war was suddenly real and warm, and this unbearable parting and coming together in the dark, confined spaces was worth all the suffering and boredom and fear.'

None of this feeling had I yet sensed when a fat man introduced himself to me, unprompted, from across the table where I was working in the Wiener Library. 'I am Sefton Delmer,' he said. 'I bet you have never heard of me. Yet I have sat as close to Adolf Hitler and to Winston Churchill as you are to me now.' It was a fine opening line, particularly from a thundering asthmatic, and it led me to read *Black Boomerang*, which is Delmer's own account of the work of the black propaganda units which he directed through most of the Second World War. This book provided the factual basis for *Licking Hitler*, and certain sections of the film do no more than recreate particular campaigns which Delmer originated, the most eccentric of which, although colourful, I omitted on the grounds that it was beyond me to make them convincing. Delmer himself, who is not represented, never saw the film, for he had a stroke a couple of months before it was shown. I had anyway chosen not to show him the script, since I took a less playful view of the unit's activities than he had done. To me they seemed to speak not just of England then but of England now.

Wise friends have told me that I should have left the metaphor alone, and that the last part of the film in which I bring the lives of the central characters up to date is the weakest. It is certainly the clumsiest in execution and, given the chance again, I would stomp through the years with less heavy boots. But I cannot concede that the intention was wrong. To me the story is not finished until you see that years later both Anna Seaton and Archie Maclean are trapped in myths about their own past from which they seem unwilling to escape. This theme serves me again in *Plenty*, but even in *Licking Hitler* it infuriated people, who asked how I could allow so fine a heroine to grow so convincingly through her wartime experience and yet be shown years later to have become effectively a victim of it. I have got used to the clamour for a simpler morality.

In the same way, feminists have been unkind to the film for its portrayal of a woman who chooses to go on meeting and making love to a man who has originally taken her by rape. They object that although such things do regrettably happen, it is the duty of responsible writers not to show them happening, and particularly via a medium which for the rest of the evening will be reinforcing the most abject sexual stereotypes. I cannot accept this argument, for to portray only what you would like to be true is the beginning of censorship. In addition Anna, however flawed, *is* the conscience of the play. In *Knuckle* the issue of conscience is much clearer. Jenny sees bad things done and condemns them, but she herself is not much changed. Increasingly in *Licking Hitler* and *Plenty* I found myself concerned with the cost of having a conscience. The clearest way I can describe *Plenty* is as a play about the cost of spending your whole life in dissent.

All three of these heroines were played by Kate Nelligan, whose Canadian background always seemed to suit the parts well. A strange misunderstanding once came about between us when I was directing her in a scene and explained that some short phrase or other was intended coldly. 'It's just manners', I said. She could not understand what I was getting at, for to her manners meant no more than the art of being polite, whereas I, of course, being English, took manners to be a kind of formalized hostility, a way of being distant. 'Thank you very much,' we say, meaning 'That's enough of that.' This kind of code is second nature to me, but Kate had to learn it and observe it as a foreigner. She approached the part of Anna Seaton as anthropology, and her performance has strengths of observation which fit well with Bill Paterson's remarkable Archie Maclean.

Licking Hitler stirred up people's memories, and many wrote to me about their direct experience of a landscape I had only imagined. I have rarely been happier than in the days I spent before shooting when I went to interview at first hand as many of the original black propaganda teams as I could find. Travelling such distances, it was hard not to feel that these people had literally been cast aside. I was in Cornwall one day, Edinburgh another, to meet men and women whose lives were publicly neglected and forgotten and whose original intense experience had long been lost. War brings together those who would not otherwise meet; that is its whole appeal. But then it sends them away.

We filmed in Compton Verney, a fine country house which had once served as a lunatic asylum. I had never looked down a camera until the first day of shooting. This was my own secret, which I only revealed later in the week. I think the crew actually enjoyed carrying a novice, teaching me as we went along. As far as I was concerned, the film was already shot in my head. The editing was only a formality. We simply strung together what we had, and there was the film, like a mosaic. I think we threw away barely thirty shots. This method of making films is fine when it works but of course is highly dangerous because you have no safety net. If in the editing a sequence turns out to be misconceived, then you have no spare material to play around with, as I was to find out two years later, when I launched into *Dreams of Leaving* with a confidence which turned out to be misplaced.

Summer came as we worked; the make-up girls picnicked by the lake; and Bill Paterson, fieldglasses round his neck, went bird-watching in his dressing gown, like Chaplin, alone in the Warwickshire woods.

I wrote *Plenty* alongside *Licking Hitler*, and because I directed them both as well, the different stages of their execution are lost to me. I know that some days I would spend the morning writing *Plenty* and the afternoon in the cutting-room with *Licking Hitler*. Made up of similar elements, they have, however, very different emphases, one concentrating on the war, the other on the peace. I had originally been attracted by a statistic, which I now cannot place, that 75 per cent of the women flown behind the lines for the Special Operations Executive were subsequently divorced after the war. The person who has had a good war and then can find no role in the peace is, of course, a character who has often been written before, perhaps best by Terence Rattigan, whose Freddy in *The Deep Blue Sea* is a brilliantly realized part. But I also had the wider aim of trying to set one character's life against the days of English plenty.

In England the opposition to *Plenty* forms around the feeling that from the start Susan Traherne contains the seeds of her own destruction, and that the texture of the society in which she happens to live is nearly irrelevant, for she is bent on objecting to it, whatever its qualities. This was certainly not what I intended, yet I can see that in the English theatre the counter-balance of the play, which is Brock's destruction, does go comparatively unremarked because it is the kind of death so many members of the audience have chosen, a death by compromise and absorption into institutional life. I intend to show the struggle of a heroine against a deceitful and emotionally stultified class, yet some sections of the English audience miss this, for they see what Susan is up against as life itself.

I became much more acutely aware of this when I revived the play in New York, four years after its original production at the National Theatre in 1978. The play proved to be a lot less controversial in America and enjoyed a breadth of approval which I had never known at home. In part this was no doubt because the American audience felt themselves much less implicated in the play's judgements. Although they found parallels with their own lives in the movement of the play—elaborate analogies were drawn with the American experience in Vietnam—they enjoyed the sense of seeing things at one remove. But they were also, of course, not afraid to look English society in the eye, to see Suez as criminal and the Foreign Office as absurd. They also seemed less frightened of a strong woman.

Many people who had seen both productions congratulated me on my rewriting, especially of the second act. But I had done no rewriting except to change four lines whose references were too local. Why, then, did the play seem clearer? Why did the second act, which had previously seemed jerky and erratic, seem now to play through cleanly to its end? The only answer I have is time. Somehow time itself had solved the play's problems and put it in a perspective which helped it. Although we had meddled with the play's interpretation—Susan was a less isolated figure at the beginning than in the London production—most of our work had been done for us, by something over which we had no control. I cannot explain this phenomenon any further.

More and more I feel writers have little idea of what they are writing. However much they exercise control by will, they remain for years ignorant of the true subject of their own work. Lately, attending a performance of *Teeth 'n' Smiles* which I had written in 1975, I was astonished by an incident in the plot which came directly from my own life and yet which at the time of writing had not then yet happened to me. From my point of view, the idea of putting these three plays together in one volume will be for me to have one more go at rooting out my confusions; from yours, I hope it will be to give pleasure.

D.H.
August 1983

Knuckle

I had to admit that I lived for nights like these, moving across the city's great broken body making connections among its millions of cells. I had a crazy wish or fantasy that some day before I died, if I had all the right neural connections, the city would come all the way alive. Like the Bride of Frankenstein.

Ross Macdonald

Characters

CURLY DELAFIELD
JENNY WILBUR
GRACE DUNNING
PATRICK DELAFIELD
MAX DUPREE
BARMAN
STOREMAN
POLICEMAN
PORTER
THE MICHAEL LOMAX TRIO

Knuckle was first presented by Michael Codron at the Comedy Theatre, London, on 4 March 1974. The cast was as follows:

CURLY DELAFIELD	Edward Fox
JENNY WILBUR	Kate Nelligan
GRACE DUNNING	Shelagh Fraser
PATRICK DELAFIELD	Douglas Wilmer
MAX DUPREE	Malcolm Storry
BARMAN	Leonard Kavanagh
STOREMAN	David Jones
POLICEMAN	Stephen Gordon
PORTER	
THE MICHAEL LOMAX TRIO	

Director	Michael Blakemore
Settings	John Napier
Music	Marc Wilkinson

The main set is the Shadow of the Moon Club. The changes from scene to scene must always be very fast indeed. For this reason it is wiser not to drop a curtain between each scene.

Time—the present.

Knuckle

PART I

SCENE I

The Shadow of the Moon Club. Night.
  There is a long, low bar; also a table, chairs and stools.
  When the curtain rises, JENNY *is sitting at a table, drinking and smoking.*
The BARMAN, *Tom, is behind the bar.* LOMAX's *voice is heard on the loudspeakers.*

LOMAX: (*Off*) Ladies and Gentlemen, dance to the music of
  Michael Lomax and the Freshman Three.
  (*A hick band starts playing 'String of Pearls', thin and distant.*
  CURLY *strides into the bar.*)
CURLY: I'm having a lemonade.
BARMAN: Fresh lemon, sir?
CURLY: Fresh lemon.
  (*The* BARMAN *sets to.* JENNY *goes up to* CURLY.)
JENNY: Is your name Curly?
CURLY: (*Points to a table.*) Just a moment.
JENNY: Hullo.
CURLY: And a Scotch.
  (JENNY *goes and sits down. The* BARMAN *holds the glass against an*
  upside-down whisky bottle.)
  Bottle.
BARMAN: Sir?
CURLY: I want to look at the bottle.
  (*The* BARMAN *hands over the bottle.* CURLY *unscrews the measuring*
  top and takes a wet wad out of it.)
  Blotting paper. That's a terrible trick.
BARMAN: Sir.
CURLY: If you do that again I'll squeeze the lemon in your eye.
BARMAN: Sir.

CURLY: And now I'll have the bottle.

(*He carries the bottle over to* JENNY*'s table and puts it down.* JENNY *gives the* BARMAN *a nod. The* BARMAN *exits.*)

Got you a drink.

JENNY: Thank you.

(*Pause.*)

You look like your sister.

CURLY: The Shadow of the Moon. Is this still the only club in Guildford?

(*He sits at the table.*)

JENNY: This is it.

CURLY: Did Sarah come here?

JENNY: You know Sarah?

CURLY: No, I don't. That's the whole point. I hadn't seen her for twelve years. I haven't seen anyone.

JENNY: What made you come back?

CURLY: Was she friendly with men?

JENNY: In a way. She went for a particular kind . . .

CURLY: I remember.

JENNY: You know . . .

CURLY: Still the same kind?

JENNY: These had a kind of Neanderthal gleam.

CURLY: That's them. And she was only eight at the time.

JENNY: Did your father ask you to do this?

CURLY: Where was she working?

JENNY: She'd been working as a nurse in a psychiatric hospital.

CURLY: Dangerous job.

JENNY: Have you seen your father?

CURLY: Not yet. I'm staying with Patrick from tonight.

JENNY: I see.

CURLY: How long's she been gone?

JENNY: You take your conversation at a fair old lick.

CURLY: I'm transistorized. How long's she been gone?

(JENNY *insists on a pause.*)

JENNY: (*Stubbing out her cigarette*) Eight weeks.

CURLY: Where exactly did she disappear?

JENNY: Between Eastbourne and Pevensey Bay there's a stretch

of beach about a mile long. Just dune and shingle. It's
called the Crumbles.

CURLY: Had she been to Eastbourne before?

JENNY: I don't know.

CURLY: What do the police have to say?

JENNY: They think if she did drown herself in Eastbourne it
would be six weeks yet before she was washed up in Herne
Bay. A tribute to the strength of the English Channel.

CURLY: And Sarah's extraordinary buoyancy. Have a cigarette.

JENNY: No, thank you.

CURLY: Was she suicidal?

JENNY: I don't know what it means.

CURLY: Down in the dumps.

(*He puts down the cigarettes. He never smokes himself.*)

JENNY: She was a paranoid. Of a particularly lethal type.

CURLY: Go on.

JENNY: I know you don't like me, she used to say. Begging you
to say, of course I like you. If you didn't say that, she was
finished. And if you did say it, she didn't believe you. And
once she couldn't believe that she couldn't believe
anything. Everything you said had black wings and a
bloodstained beak.

CURLY: And she was the nurse.

JENNY: Yes.

CURLY: Have a cigarette?

JENNY: No, thank you.

(*She deliberately lights her own cigarette.*)

CURLY: But not what you'd call suicidal.

JENNY: She was depressed. So. Everyone's depressed. She used
to say life was a plush abattoir. Fair enough.

CURLY: Fair enough.

JENNY: She used to say—this is a very pretentious girl—she used
to say she'd recognize a moment of happiness because—she
remembered having one in 1965, and if another came
along, she could compare.

CURLY: When was that?

JENNY: Don't know. One evening, before dusk. She felt happy.

For about twenty minutes . . .

CURLY: Well . . .

JENNY: Well—what she said—more than her fair share.
(*Pause. The music ends, followed by clapping.*)

CURLY: Special friends, did she have?

JENNY: A journalist called Dupree.

CURLY: Who else?

JENNY: Just me.

CURLY: Like her pretty well?

JENNY: Pretty well.

CURLY: Have another drink.

JENNY: No.

CURLY: Not happy. Not liked. Pretentious.

JENNY: We all told her she was pretentious. And she said
certainly I am. That's because the world is unduly modest.

CURLY: Yes, well, there you are.

JENNY: You left home much earlier she said.

CURLY: When I was fifteen.

JENNY: She said you took four dozen rifles from the school cadet
corps and sold them to the IRA.

CURLY: Old story. Not necessarily true.

JENNY: Then sold the IRA to the British police.

CURLY: That sounds more like me. I was—loud. Had the second
half of the pint. That sort of thing. Smoked twenty a day.
But I've quietened down.

LOMAX: (*Off, over the mike*) It's Hawaiian night in the Paradise
Room.
(CURLY *gets up and helps himself to lemonade from behind the bar.*)
(*Off*) Grass skirts, sweet music, and good food. The
Paradise Room is situated on the first floor, just beyond
William Tell's Alpine Grotto. Hurry up to Heaven.
(*A xylophonist starts playing 'Under a Blanket of Blue'.* JENNY
does not look at CURLY *behind her.*)

JENNY: Are you afraid?

CURLY: Why?

JENNY: If she was dead does that frighten you?

CURLY: I'm not afraid.

JENNY: They found a purse on the beach. And a coat. Which is how they know she was there. And inside the purse they found two railway tickets. Returns to Victoria. Which means she was with someone. Which may mean she was killed.

CURLY: Is that consistent?

JENNY: What?

CURLY: Is that consistent with how she lived?

JENNY: Sarah? Sure. Like all women. Hanging out for it . . .

CURLY: All right.

JENNY: Longs to be raped. Is that not what you think?

CURLY: All right.

JENNY: Well . . .

 (*Pause.*)

CURLY: Did she live with you?

JENNY: The machine grinds on.

CURLY: Did she live with you?

JENNY: She moved into my flat. She left Guildford to avoid her father. She ran away to Surbiton. Don't laugh. She couldn't gesture as big as you. Venezuela, wherever it was . . .

CURLY: Peru . . .

JENNY: She ran away to Surbiton. That's the scale of her life.

CURLY: Had she been to Eastbourne before?

JENNY: It's nice to hear the old ones again.

CURLY: Had she been to Eastbourne before?

JENNY: Often.

CURLY: Why?

JENNY: You could breathe in Eastbourne. That's what she said.

CURLY: You didn't tell me that before.

JENNY: I was waiting for you to uncurl your lip.

CURLY: That's how I keep it. Catches crumbs. What do you do for a living?

JENNY: I manage this club.

CURLY: Who owns it?

JENNY: A man called Malloy. Runs it on the side.

CURLY: What else does he do?

JENNY: What does everyone do in Guildford?

CURLY: Work in the City.

JENNY: City. Right.

CURLY: Friend of Sarah's?

JENNY: Friend of us all. This is our home.

CURLY: I used to come here . . .

JENNY: Yes?

CURLY: It was skiffle. In my day. One time I . . .

JENNY: Pissed in a bottle and made them sell it as Martini.

CURLY: You knew.

JENNY: You're a legend.

CURLY: Sold like a bomb.

JENNY: It's changed since then. It used to be the club of clubs.
We all came here. Young Guildford, with our coke and
benzedrine. For a lot of us it was paradise. Loud and
lovely. Then it lost its way. The lushes moved in and the
middle-aged voyeurs. Now it's just a bomb site. Well, you
can see . . .

CURLY: Why do you stay?

JENNY: Not your business.

CURLY: I'm asking.

JENNY: Do you know what Sarah said about you . . . ?

CURLY: Nice girl.

JENNY: She said whenever you stood up there were two greasy
patches on the seat of your chair.

(*Pause. The music ends, followed by clapping.*)

CURLY: I'm here for her sake. That's all.

JENNY: Nobody asked you.

CURLY: And now I'm here I won't be put off. Nobody told me,
do you know? I read it for myself, in an English paper. I
reckon I'm far enough away from you all—

JENNY: Don't count me . . .

CURLY: —to be the best person to find out what happened. I
hold no brief for the Home Counties. Nor its inhabitants.

JENNY: Best left to the police.

CURLY: They don't have my equipment. The steel-tipped boot,
you know, the knuckleduster.

JENNY: I can tell you've been out of the country.

LOMAX: (*Off*) Ladies and gentlemen, for each and everyone of us there must surely come the day when—we'll gather lilacs.
　　(*The band plays a reedy introduction to 'We'll Gather Lilacs'.*)

CURLY: Dance?

JENNY: Dance with you?

CURLY: It's that or go home to my father.

JENNY: You're squat and ugly.

CURLY: I am repulsive. That is true.
　　(*Pause.*)

JENNY: Well, there you are.

CURLY: What I say is: don't piss in the well. One day you may want to drink from it.
　　(CURLY *stands.* JENNY *begins to dance with him at arm's length. The music swells to very loud.*)

SCENE 2

The drawing-room of the Guildford house, Delafields'. Night.
　Everything is just so. As the curtain rises, MRS DUNNING *is sitting on the sofa, sorting clothes from a box on the floor into a suitcase on the coffee table. She is Scottish.*
　CURLY *comes through the door.*

CURLY: Good evening. We haven't met yet. My name is Curly. Patrick's son Curly.

MRS DUNNING: They let you into the country all right?

CURLY: No trouble. Where's Pa?

MRS DUNNING: Upstairs.

CURLY: Have you lived here long?

MRS DUNNING: About a year.
　　(CURLY *fingers casually through a pile of clothes.*)

CURLY: There seems very little point in storing clothes—

MRS DUNNING: Yes . . .

CURLY: —that are well past wearing.
　　(*He holds up an article of clothing.*)

27

MRS DUNNING: That's a gymslip.

CURLY: She was twenty-one. White socks and a nice school blouse.

MRS DUNNING: Excuse me.
   (*She goes to the door.*)
   Patrick. Somebody to see you.

CURLY: Your son.

MRS DUNNING: I've given you your old room.
   (*She sits again.*)

CURLY: Ah, next to the boiler.

MRS DUNNING: Your father is greatly looking forward to seeing you.
   (*Pause.*)
   Patrick is a very Christian man.
   (PATRICK *swings the door open.*)

PATRICK: Curly. How wonderful. How good to see you.

CURLY: I'm over here.

PATRICK: Of course you are.
   (*Pause.*)
   Well, *Chara en thlipsae*. In the heart of sadness joy. Sit down.

CURLY: Thank you.
   (*He sits.*)

PATRICK: Have you met Mrs Dunning?

CURLY: Yes, indeed.

PATRICK: Grace as we call her. I mean, that's her name. Grace.

CURLY: Sits pretty.

PATRICK: Good.
   (*He sits. Pause.*)

CURLY: Pa . . .

PATRICK: Let me . . .

CURLY: The limits of the visit must be firmly set. You're the second on a list of people I'm to see.

PATRICK: Fine.

CURLY: I saw Jenny.

PATRICK: Nice girl.

CURLY: Yes.

PATRICK: A brightly painted object.

CURLY: So tell me what you know.

PATRICK: It was good of you to come.

CURLY: I was between wars. I was happy to come.

PATRICK: As you say.

CURLY: Well?

PATRICK: I only know what you've read in the paper. They say fifteen thousand Englishmen disappear every year—are never seen again. Amazing.

CURLY: But this is different.

PATRICK: Because she disappeared by the seashore. Not the kind of place where people disappear.

CURLY: She'd had a row with you . . .

PATRICK: That was a year ago.

CURLY: She'd left home.

PATRICK: A year ago. She was twenty-one. She was bound to leave.

CURLY: What were the reasons?

PATRICK: Curly, take the light bulb out of my eyes. Goodness me. Let's take it a little more slowly.

CURLY: She was suicidal.

PATRICK: Who says that?

(CURLY *gets up*.)

CURLY: (*To* MRS DUNNING) He can't be trusted. He drops people like eggs.

(*He picks up a photo of Sarah as a young girl from a shelf*.)

PATRICK: I'm not expected to run her life for her.

MRS DUNNING: (*Holding it up*) Exercise book.

PATRICK: That would have been quite wrong.

MRS DUNNING: (*Reading*) 'Ah bonjour Monsieur le Corbeau que vous me semblez beau.'

(*Pause*.)

CURLY: Tell me the truth.

PATRICK: She wasn't impressed with my profession. The merchant bank. She didn't care much for yours, either.

CURLY: No.

PATRICK: But it's more glamorous than just making money.

CURLY: *Just* making money?

PATRICK: (*Smiling*) I'm trying to see it from her point of view. (*Pause.*)

CURLY: Is that why she left?

PATRICK: I suppose.

CURLY: It wasn't more personal? (*Pause.*) Had you spoken since she left?

PATRICK: Not really.

CURLY: The days I knew her she was brought up like an orchid.

PATRICK: Well . . .

CURLY: That's how she was cast.

MRS DUNNING: Perhaps that was the trouble.

CURLY: What?

PATRICK: There isn't any trouble. She is highly strung. Like many of her generation without the broader-based values . . .

CURLY: Of a traditional education.

(*He replaces the photograph.*)

PATRICK: She was unsure of herself.

CURLY: Did she threaten to kill herself?

(*Pause.*)

PATRICK: She was self-critical, as you know. She thought she was a hateful kind of a person. She used to say she had contracted one of Surrey's contagious diseases—moral gumrot, internal decay. Well, that's easy to say. She could say it. But nobody else. That's the point. So here we have paranoia. The fear of other people pointing out to you what you've been saying all the time about yourself, much louder, much longer.

MRS DUNNING: (*Still storing.*) I wonder if Alice bands will ever come back into fashion again.

CURLY: And you?

PATRICK: What?

CURLY: What did you think?

PATRICK: I thought it was rather lame propaganda. (*Pause.*) Mrs Dunning, I think we could afford a cup of tea.

MRS DUNNING: Of course.

(*She rises and closes the suitcase.*)

PATRICK: Not for me.

CURLY: Really?

PATRICK: I always have mine at half past four.

CURLY: It's a quarter to midnight.

PATRICK: Another would be decadence. Right, Mrs D?

MRS DUNNING: Fine.

CURLY: Mrs Dunning. Use my father's old tea bag, if you like.
(MRS DUNNING *goes out with the suitcase*.)

PATRICK: Curly, you don't change.

CURLY: I recur.

PATRICK: Curly . . .

CURLY: Uh. Business, Father. Nothing at the human level,
please. After all these years it would be hard to take.
Just—tell me what you said to Sarah.
(*Pause*.)

PATRICK: I've always thought that life was—volatile. You should
tread light. It's not a point of view Sarah could understand.
I think everyone's entitled to their own illusions. Sarah
thought not. Sarah thought everyone should know
everything. She told the Bishop of Guildford that his son
was known as Mabel and the toast of the Earls Court Road.

CURLY: I see.

PATRICK: She said it was best he should know.

CURLY: What does she look like?

PATRICK: She's thin and angular. Wears grubby white jeans. Her
hair always as if she's just been caught in a blaze. And the
same expression of shock. All bones and big lips. Does that
help?

CURLY: I . . .

PATRICK: How long since you saw her?

CURLY: Twelve years. Since I saw either of you.
(*Pause*.)

PATRICK: I hadn't seen her for six months. She went to live with
Jenny. Then one day the police came to my door.

CURLY: Do you think she's dead?

PATRICK: I do rather. It's my experience of life that it never
misses a trick. And murdered as well. I expect. (*Pause*.) She

31

was like a buzz-saw in the inner ear. (*Pause.*) Some
man she talked to on the beach.

CURLY: What about the police?

PATRICK: That's the current theory. There's apparently a
man—well-known in Eastbourne—called Dawson. Known
as Dopey. Always out on the street. Reads the Bible to
children. Shows them the meat hook he keeps in his mac.
Used to be borough surveyor. Some years ago.

CURLY: Is there any evidence?

PATRICK: Lord, no, no evidence. Sounds rather easy but it's all
they've got.

CURLY: There's a boyfriend . . .

PATRICK: Dupree . . .

CURLY: Yeah.

PATRICK: Not the right type . . .

CURLY: Not the right type for Sarah, eh?

PATRICK: Curly, you know better than that. Not the right type to
kill, I meant.

CURLY: Which type is that?

PATRICK: Dupree is a remarkably fine young man.

CURLY: Solid sort of chap.

PATRICK: As you say.

CURLY: Must have been great for Sarah.

PATRICK: Well . . .

CURLY: (*Breaking*) Pa . . .

PATRICK: The police visit me every night at eight. I will of course
pass on to you everything they discover to help
your—private search for justice . . .

CURLY: It's not justice I'm after.

PATRICK: I wish you well.

CURLY: Then tell me the truth. What about the club? The man
that owns it—Malloy. Do you know him?

PATRICK: Of course. Stockbroker. Not very successful. His hands
tremble. It's—bad for business.

CURLY: Is that why he bought the club?

PATRICK: I should think so. He's almost my age, but he seems to
enjoy the company of—young people.

CURLY: And what does that mean?

PATRICK: Curly . . .

CURLY: Why did Sarah leave home? Tell me why she left.

PATRICK: (*Good-humouredly*) Life with Sarah was constant self-justification. I don't propose to start all over with you.

CURLY: When did the Scots haddock arrive?

PATRICK: Grace . . .

CURLY: The smell of starch and clean living when you come in that door . . .

PATRICK: Mrs Dunning . . .

CURLY: I bet she dabs Dettol behind her ears.

PATRICK: She wasn't here then.

CURLY: I'd have left home if I saw that coming. I can sympathize. This place is like silver paper between your teeth. I'm back five minutes and I'm . . .

PATRICK: As before.

(*Pause.*)

CURLY: (*Quietly*) Don't cross your legs. It spoils the crease.

(*Pause.*)

PATRICK: Mrs Dunning is a pillar of strength. The best housekeeper I've had. You can say anything at all to her. Anything you like. Grace, you have a very large mouth and very small heart. You could say that. She wouldn't mind. If it were true you could say that. Which it's not.

CURLY: Punchbag, eh?

PATRICK: Do you think, Curly, while you're here, a guest in my home, you could suppress the all-singing, all-dancing, all-fornicating side of your character which burst out so tellingly before you left—we do hope you've grown up.

(MRS DUNNING *enters with a laden tray.*)

MRS DUNNING: I did know you were coming.

PATRICK: Matured.

MRS DUNNING: I was told to get walnut whips. Your father said you loved . . .

CURLY: Yes, well . . .

MRS DUNNING: Walnut whips.

PATRICK: I wasn't saying we should have them today.

MRS DUNNING: You emphasized the point.

PATRICK: It was twelve years ago. After all . . .

CURLY: Mrs Dunning . . . (*Pause.*) You have a very large
mouth . . .

MRS DUNNING: (*With great pleasure*) And a very small heart. That's
what your father always says.
(*She sits and pours tea.*)

PATRICK: I think I must be going to bed.
(*He rises.*)

CURLY: You haven't told me about Sarah.

PATRICK: There's plenty of time.

CURLY: You do want me to help?

PATRICK: Curly, I do indeed. Indeed I do.

CURLY: Then that's what I shall do. Help and then go.

PATRICK: Excellent (*Pause.*) We'll wait and see if you measure
up.

CURLY: Pa . . .

PATRICK: Ah—we'll talk more tomorrow. Grace, my Henry
James.

MRS DUNNING: By the bed.

PATRICK: (*Looking at his watch*) The light will go out at a quarter
past twelve.
(PATRICK *exits.*)

MRS DUNNING: And now we'll have a cup of tea.

CURLY: (*Dead quiet*) Sod the tea. (*Pause.*) Did you know
Sarah?

MRS DUNNING: I came after Sarah. I formed the impression of a
tremendously vital girl.

CURLY: Vital?

MRS DUNNING: She seemed to care so much about the world.

CURLY: Sarah and I went to a martello tower on Aldeburgh
beach when we were youngish—I think I was
thirteen—there was a poodle playing inside which
followed us to the top. Sarah—me—we didn't have a
great deal in common, but at that moment, together, we
simultaneously conceived the idea of throwing the poodle

34

over the side of the tower. I can't tell you why but it was a hypnotic idea. Just to see it fall. So—we lifted this grey thing up to the edge, then we released at either end, at exactly the same moment—it's the firing squad idea—you don't know who's responsible. We felt terrible.

MRS DUNNING: Worse for the dog.

CURLY: Bad for the dog. Also. But also terrible for us. The only barbaric thing I've ever done.

MRS DUNNING: You've quite a reputation as a barbarian.

CURLY: Ignorance.

MRS DUNNING: Ah.

CURLY: Ignorance and jealousy. Don't tell Pa.
    (*Pause.*)

MRS DUNNING: A wonderful man. He's undertaken an intensive study of Anglo-American literature.

CURLY: Micky Spillane.

MRS DUNNING: He's on the *Golden Bowl*. He knows an incredible amount.

CURLY: For a merchant banker.

MRS DUNNING: He's a cultured man.

CURLY: Sure he's cultured. What good does that do?

MRS DUNNING: His culture enlarges his . . .

CURLY: Mrs Dunning. Who ran Auschwitz? A pack of bloody intellectuals.

MRS DUNNING: I must go up.
    (*She rises.*)

CURLY: Is he your beau?

MRS DUNNING: You must have lived in his shadow. When you were a child.

CURLY: We thought he was a fool.

MRS DUNNING: Such a tremendously clever man.

CURLY: The trick of making money—is only a trick.

MRS DUNNING: He said he thought—you'd have grown up.
    (*She goes towards the door.*)

CURLY: Do the police always call?

MRS DUNNING: At eight o'clock. That's it. A typical evening.

Since Sarah.

(*Pause.*)

CURLY: What's he doing?

MRS DUNNING: Reading his book. (*Pause.*) Did you never like him?

CURLY: Not very much.

MRS DUNNING: I wonder why all the words my generation believed in—words like honour and loyalty—are now just a joke.

CURLY: I guess it's because of some of the characters they've knocked around with. Good night.

(*He picks up Sarah's photograph.*)

MRS DUNNING: Good night.

(*As* MRS DUNNING *turns towards the door, music—'For All We Know', with strings—fades up.*)

SCENE 3

Acton Warehouse. Day.

The stage is bare. A STOREMAN *wheels on a rack of rifles, as large and as many as possible.* CURLY *walks straight on. He takes the revolver the* STOREMAN *offers him.*

The music stops.

CURLY *takes two steps down stage. Then he aims with great care and no fuss, and fires six times at six targets just ahead into the audience. It must look perfect.*

CURLY: We'll take 2,000 Mannlicher-Carcanos, carbine and ammunition, 1,500 Tokarevs, 1,400 Mosin-Nagants, what few bolt-action Mausers you have, and the rest of the Lee-Enfields. Knock-down job lot. My client is also in the market for point thirty-o-six Springfield rifles with extra long chrome-plated bayonets. Believe it or not. And he'd also like an antique Mauser Nazi 'K' series Luger for himself. As he's a bit of a raving lunatic on the side.

(CURLY *stuffs a green wadge of money into the* STOREMAN*'s pocket.*)
And he'll be paying cash. Swiss francs.
STOREMAN: Anything you say, Mr Delafield.
CURLY: And God help the poor bloody wogs.
(*'For All We Know' swamps the action again.*)

SCENE 4

The Hospital Grounds. Day.
   When the curtain rises the stage is in darkness except for a spot on
CURLY.

CURLY: Every man has his own gun. That's not a metaphor.
   That's a fact. There are 750 million guns in the world in
   some kind of working order. Everyone can have one like
   every German was going to get a Volkswagen. I don't pick
   the fights. I just equip them. People are going to fight
   anyway. They're going to kill each other with or without
   my help. There isn't a civilization you can name that hasn't
   operated at the most staggering cost in human life. It's as if
   we *need* so many dead—like axle grease—to make
   civilization work at all. Do you know how many people
   have died in wars this century? One hundred million. And
   how many of those before 1945? Over 95 million. These last
   twenty-five years have been among the most restrained in
   man's history. Half a million in Biafra maybe, 2 million
   perhaps in Vietnam. Pinpricks.
   (*The lights come up to reveal a stage bare except for a single bench.*
   MAX *is sitting on it, slumped forward. His face cannot be seen
   because he is staring at the ground.*)
   Things are actually getting better. The enormous
   continuing proliferation of arms since 1945 has actually led
   to a massive drop in the global numbers of dead. So there.
   I'm not ashamed of the trade, even if I'm a little tired of it.

If every man on earth has a gun already, does he really
need a second one? So now we can talk.

MAX: I asked Jenny what's his attitude to his profession, and she
said—well, he says every man has his own gun, that's not a
metaphor, that's a fact.

CURLY: It's my party piece. You sell guns, people come up to
you. They can spot a moral issue. And I'm a tissue of moral
issues. Like having a very loud suit. You get used to it.

MAX: OK.

CURLY: I have to get the subject out of the way.

MAX: OK. (*Pause.*) Well, she worked over there. In that lovely
old house. And by all accounts was a very fine nurse.

CURLY: What would you say was wrong with her?

MAX: Why does there have to be something wrong? Sarah was
unhappy, that's all. She needed character massage.

CURLY: She wasn't ill?

MAX: Ill?

CURLY: Mentally?

MAX: I've written stories about this hospital for the national
newspapers. One about a man who wrapped his hands in
copper wire and plugged himself into the mains. Another
who believes there's a colony of rats lodged in his stomach
wall. He drinks Domestos. Friend. So if a girl's unhappy
because her father sits smiling all day with his arse in a
bucket of cream, and because she thinks her brother's a
twenty-four carat shark, I don't get very worked up. As far
as I'm concerned she's just ambling round the foothills of
the thing, and is unlikely to come to very much harm.

CURLY: (*Sitting beside* MAX) Is that true? About why she was
unhappy?

MAX: Certainly . . .

CURLY: I'd heard she was living with you.

MAX: (*Smiling*) Neanderthal type.

CURLY: Well?

MAX: She stopped over.

CURLY: Lucky girl.

MAX: She was free.

CURLY: Do you think she's run away?

MAX: No, I don't.

CURLY: Do you think she's killed herself?

MAX: I don't understand your involvement.

CURLY: I'm her brother.

MAX: I thought she was just axle grease . . .

CURLY: This is different . . .

MAX: Make civilization work . . .

CURLY: You think she killed herself . . .

MAX: Mr Delafield . . ..

CURLY: Mr Dupree . . . (*Pause.*) One shark to another: tell me the truth.

MAX: I'm not a shark. (*Rising to behind the bench*) And I don't think she killed herself. (*Pause.*) But, of course, she had threatened it.

CURLY: Go on.

MAX: She wasn't quite mature. She had a misleading reputation. She was known as Legover Sarah. That was fine by me. But it wasn't true. In fact she was more possessive than she appeared. She blackmailed me—(*He smiles, embarrassed*)—by saying she would kill herself. If I left her.

CURLY: Well . . .

MAX: So.

CURLY: Quite a man, Mr Dupree.

MAX: She was immature.

CURLY: Sure. Sure.

MAX: It was a terrific responsibility.

CURLY: Sure.

MAX: So when I first heard she'd disappeared I was terrified. But as soon as I heard about the purse . . .

CURLY: Of course.

MAX: Two railway tickets on the beach . . .

CURLY: Right.

MAX: I knew she couldn't have killed herself.

CURLY: So that's all right. (*Pause.*) It's beautiful here.

MAX: It's a lovely place to go mad. There's a woman in there who thinks she's Napoleon.

CURLY: Sure. That I can understand. But who the hell did
Napoleon think he was?
(MAX *smiles*.)
Mr Dupree, I'm told you're a Communist. What would you
say?

MAX: Not a Communist exactly.

CURLY: That sort of thing.

MAX: Certainly.

CURLY: And you lived with Sarah . . .

MAX: Off and on . . .

CURLY: While entertaining other women . . .

MAX: That's true.

CURLY: Fair enough. I'm not accusing you. It seems a
reasonable way of life.

MAX: Well?

CURLY: I just don't understand why a middle-aged, god-loving
merchant banker should describe the lazy, promiscuous,
self-righteous bolshevik who's meanwhile screwing his
daughter as 'a remarkably fine young man'.

MAX: No.

CURLY: No.

MAX: Perhaps Patrick just liked me.
(*He moves away*.)

CURLY: Max, what's happened to Malloy?

MAX: What?

CURLY: The owner of the club, Malloy, what's happened to him?

MAX: I don't know.

CURLY: Why would it be he doesn't answer his door? And where
was he on the night Sarah disappeared? Where is he now?
Where indeed were you? Do you have an alibi?

MAX: Of course.

CURLY: All good questions. Plus: how does Jenny come into this?

MAX: Sarah's best friend, that's all.

CURLY: Not bad looking, Jenny.

MAX: If you say so . . .

CURLY: Oh, Max . . .

MAX: Nothing to do with me.

CURLY: Max. You and me. (*He gestures around him.*) The real
world. And Jennifer. You're not saying you've missed Jennifer.
The one with the legs. And the incandescent vagina. You of all
people—Max—must have noticed. Being so intelligent. And
ambitious. Yet choosing to go on living in this town, when you
don't have to. Letting yourself become the Guildford stringer.
Tying yourself down. Why would that be? Maximillian?

MAX: Maxwell.

CURLY: Max.

MAX: (*Sitting*) Jenny and Sarah. Of course one would see them
side by side. An unfair comparison. Jenny so bright and
capable and lovely. Sarah ungainly with a slight
moustache. And politically—erratic, I would say, an
emotional kind of conviction. Whereas Jenny soars above
us all. Just—beautiful. We all grew up together, went to the
same club. Sniffed the same glue. Aspirins in the Pepsi, and
French kissing. But Sarah was always—loss leader. And
I'm afraid it seems to fit that she was killed. No doubt by
some frightfully maladjusted person. (*Pause.*) And I promise
you that's what I really think.

CURLY: I don't doubt your account.

MAX: Thank you.

CURLY: I just doubt the intense sense of relief with which you tell
it. (*Pause.*) I'll see you tomorrow. Same time. Same place.

MAX: I . . .

CURLY: Tomorrow.

    (MAX *goes out.*)

    (*Alone*) You chew all the meat until you hit the lump of gristle.

SCENE 5

The Delafields' drawing-room. Night.
    PATRICK *is sitting reading a sheet of music.* CURLY *comes in.*

CURLY: I've been to see Max Dupree.

PATRICK: Come in, come in. I'm reading some most enjoyable music.

CURLY: Great.

PATRICK: The horns have just come in. Would you like a drink?

CURLY: Do you want to know what Dupree said?

PATRICK: I have an idea.

CURLY: It's all right. He's very hopeful. He hopes she was murdered. Everyone hopes that. Including you. (*Pause.*) Not because you want her dead. I didn't say that. But given that she's dead you want her murdered because then it's nobody's fault except some poor psychopath and there's nothing anyone can do about those. Whereas if she killed herself she's going to squat on your shoulders for the rest of your life.

(*Pause.*)

PATRICK: Have a drink.

(*He rises.*)

CURLY: Never touch it. Time?

PATRICK: Ten to. The police will be here at eight. Are you staying?

CURLY: I'll stay—as long as I can.

PATRICK: You're living here . . .

CURLY: I know, but I couldn't last an evening. It's—what—not yet eight and already I'm half the man I am . . .

PATRICK: It's just lack of practice. If we tried . . .

CURLY: Sure . . .

PATRICK: Sitting together . . .

CURLY: Sure . . .

PATRICK: Having a normal conversation . . .

CURLY: Sure . . .

PATRICK: Behaving normally . . .

CURLY: As if I hadn't been away twelve years.

PATRICK: Quite so. Ten minutes to eight.

CURLY: OK.

(*Pause. He takes off his coat and moves to sit.*)

I'd be pressed—Father—to put my finger on the quality that makes you impossible to spend an evening with . . .

PATRICK: That subject's taboo. Anything else . . .

CURLY: For God's sake . . .

   (*He moves to leave.*)

PATRICK: Sit down.

   (CURLY *sits.*)

Have you read much Henry James? *Washington Square.*

CURLY: No.

PATRICK: Tremendous quality of civilization.

CURLY: That's what it is. (*Pause.*) I'm not getting very far. The man. The girl. And the father. She turns out to be a hysterical kind of person whom nobody likes. Least of all Max, who's meant to be the boyfriend. There's none of the innocence that word suggests. In fact an outright narcissist. And in love with Jenny I would say. Because he thought they would look good together. Walking past mirrors, that sort of thing. I don't think he enjoyed having to make do with Sarah. I should think he winced every time she opened her mouth. For myself I'd like to meet Malloy. As he must have seen Sarah every night in the club. But Malloy, everybody, has disappeared. Time?

PATRICK: Bit later.

CURLY: Yes, my friends, vanished. My day spent battering at his door. But he has gone.

PATRICK: What's gun-running like?

CURLY: (*Rising*) For Christ's sake.

PATRICK: Sit down. I'm asking.

CURLY: I don't run them. I sell them. It's a perfectly legal profession. Like selling insurance.

PATRICK: Is there a great deal of travel?

CURLY: Lots. I was in Acton today.

PATRICK: Acton?

CURLY: There are 150,000 guns in Acton, west London. A warehouse off the A40.

PATRICK: I always thought you were in Peru.

CURLY: I go where there's a war.

PATRICK: Acton?

CURLY: Or people want one.

PATRICK: I thought you were in danger.

CURLY: There's no danger. The people who supply the arms should not be confused with the soldiers. In the trade we tend to keep soldiers at some distance. They bring bad luck. There's one man—mercenary—claims a straight flush since 1939. Indo-China, Algeria, the Congo, the Yemen, Biafra, not forgetting Hitler's war—our side, of course, Cuba, South America, back to the Congo. Then Nigeria. There's a saying in the trade.

PATRICK: Yes?

CURLY: You don't stand downwind
       Of Franz Leopold von Lind.

PATRICK: I thought you said he was on our side in the Second World War.

CURLY: Eventually. (*Pause.*) Pa . . .

PATRICK: Yes?

CURLY: What do you like so much about Max?

PATRICK: Max called me. He said he'd seen you. All you've succeeded in doing is putting his back up. I'd miscalculated. Your particular talents seem quite useless in this matter.

CURLY: Listen . . .

PATRICK: You haven't grown up. You'll never grow up until you appreciate the value of tact.

CURLY: I'm off.

PATRICK: Sit down. (*Pause.*) That's typical. You've no self-control. (*Pause.*) You should be happy to sit and be humiliated.
(CURLY *moves very slightly.*)
If you wish to destroy an ant heap, you do not use dynamite.

CURLY: You read them Henry James.

PATRICK: Just so. It's a question of noise. There is a saying in our trade. Or there ought to be. In the City. The saying is: 'The exploitation of the masses should be conducted as quietly as possible.'
(CURLY *laughs slightly.*)
Quite right. I'll tell you of an incident before she left. It

made me admire—my own daughter. I don't handle money as you know. I mean, actual notes.

CURLY: Cabbage.

PATRICK: (*Trying it*) Yes, cabbage.

CURLY: Notes are cabbage. A bank is therefore a cabbage patch and a bouncing cheque is a bruised tomato.

PATRICK: Good. I had the cabbage. For various reasons—to do with Grace—I came home with two-fifty in ones.

CURLY: You had the hots in your pocket.

PATRICK: Quite. I brought them back home. I'm a romantic. I put them in the piano, played 'Scheherazade' and went to bed. The next morning they'd gone. And so had Sarah. She'd run away to Surbiton. (*Pause.*) I was furious. It was rude and messy and—loud. But last week I went to the flat for the first time. I went into the kitchen. She'd pasted them to the wall. I admired the elegance of the gesture. It was perfectly discreet. Bless her.
(*Pause.*)

CURLY: I saw a girl once in a bar in Laos, whose trick was an inverted sphincter. She smoked a cigarette through her arse. The most impressive feature was the hush. Just complete silence as this thing worked and blew and puffed. And nobody spoke. And the action itself was perfect. It summed up for me—the pleasures of the world.
(*Pause.*)

PATRICK: You get the idea.

CURLY: Do you know what Sam said?

PATRICK: Sam?

CURLY: Sam Cummings. International arms king.

PATRICK: Ah.

CURLY: Sam said to me: 'Open up. Let 'em have it.'
(PATRICK *laughs.*)
Sam said to me: 'That's what civilization was, is and will always be. Open up. Let 'em have it.'
(PATRICK *laughs again.*)
'That is why mine is the only business that will last for ever.'

PATRICK: Goodness me.

CURLY: He said that to me when I was fifteen.

(CURLY *swings round the bottle of whisky to the table in front of him.*)

See that? I like the taste of whisky. Good whisky, Dad. But that's all I like. I don't like the effect.

(*He empties his pockets.*)

Fags. Two kinds. Cigars. Sweets. Condoms.

(*He puts them all down.*)

Do you know what I say?

PATRICK: No.

CURLY: No pleasure that isn't more pleasurable for being denied.

(*He gestures at the pile.*)

Don't use any of them.

PATRICK: Goodness me.

(*Pause.*)

CURLY: I need nothing.

PATRICK: Good. You're growing up.

(*Pause.*)

CURLY: How we doing?

PATRICK: (*Looking at his watch*) Seven minutes.

CURLY: Bloody good. (*Pause.*) Did you ever talk to Sarah? After she left?

PATRICK: We met once. Neutral ground. Trafalgar Square. She took to wearing white. We had to argue things out. We talked about—no, I can't tell you . . .

CURLY: What?

PATRICK: We talked about what we believed.

CURLY: How disgusting.

PATRICK: I suppose you have to get your hands dirty sometimes.

CURLY: And what did she believe?

PATRICK: I can't remember.

CURLY: Well, no wonder, as you paid such close attention to her views . . .

PATRICK: Hush, hush. Over the top. Way over the top again. We don't know she's dead. And if she is, there's no purpose to

be served by booting your way through the local
population like a mad Hussar. This is England. Surrey. Your
approach is wrong. You're peg-legging along screaming your
head off fifteen paces behind the local police. You've no idea.
(CURLY *gets up.*)

CURLY: Jesus. I try to wipe my slate as clean as yours. Alcohol.
Sex. I have left them behind. But I still can't quite manage
your state of Zen. I still have a smudge of indignation. You
still drive me fucking mad. I left this house because I was
sick to death with Lord Earthly-bloody Perfection. If only
you'd admit . . .

PATRICK: What?

CURLY: Just—something. Just own up. For instance, to your
genius for mislaying your children.

PATRICK: Curly . . .

CURLY: I can't stand it.

PATRICK: Please.

CURLY: I thought when I came back you might be showing just
a little petticoat below your hem. But no. (*He shows.*)
Perfection. (*Pause.*) I'm clocking out. World Champion at
nine minutes. I quit the game.

(*He makes to go out.*)

PATRICK: Curly.

(CURLY *pauses.*)

Please take your condoms off my table.

(CURLY *is about to exit and the music of 'We Gather Lilacs' is
heard, as the curtain falls.*)

SCENE 6

The Shadow of the Moon bar. Night.
    JENNY *is sitting at the table, crying. The* BARMAN *is behind the bar.*
CURLY *enters and goes straight to him.*

BARMAN: The lemonade, is it, sir?

CURLY: No. Yes. I'll stick to lemonade.

BARMAN: Pleasure to serve you, Mr Delafield.

    (CURLY *just looks away.*)

    You know this can be a pretty wild bar some nights.

CURLY: Lordy.

BARMAN: A little too wild. Without a piece.

    (*Pause.* CURLY *does not answer.*)

    Oh, yes. Everyone needs a piece nowadays, eh?

CURLY: (*Half at Jenny*) Who is this creep?

BARMAN: Right, Mr Delafield.

CURLY: And a Scotch, I suppose.

BARMAN: I'm talking about a hot rod, Mr Delafield. As you call
    it in the trade. (*Pause.*) Naturally we've got the security
    boys, private army, you know. But they don't have the
    lead . . .

CURLY: No . . .

BARMAN: Perhaps you could—cross my palm with metal, Mr
    Delafield.

CURLY: Perhaps. (*He pauses, then smiles.*) Open up, let 'em have it.

BARMAN: (*Smiling*) Right, Mr Delafield.

    (CURLY *walks over to* JENNY *with the drinks.*)

CURLY: What a creep. I wouldn't sell him a water-pistol.

    (*He sets down the bottle.*)

    Well, Potato-face, your lucky day. This is Repulsive
    speaking. I am offering you a night on the tiles. What do
    you say? We could maybe both go look for Malloy.

JENNY: You can find Malloy. Down the mortuary. (*Pause.*) The
    wrists are cut. With the razor blade. Not easy. You really
    have to go at them. He went at them. So it looked like
    gardening shears. The only way to do it.

    (*Pause.*)

CURLY: Jen.

JENNY: Who the hell am I? I bet you don't even know my second
    name.

    (*Pause.*)

CURLY: Have another Scotch.

JENNY: What's it to you? (*Pause.*) So that is why he does not answer the door. Because he is lying on the floor. With a suicide note. Bequeathing me the Shadow of the Moon. (*Pause.*) Malloy had ears like a dachshund. And a voice like two trees rubbing together. In short, a slob. He liked to put a brown paper bag over his head—this will amuse you —then take all his clothes off. He did this in the company of other Englishmen of the same age and class. They ran round in circles. With straps. They never saw each others' faces. Malloy said—the pleasure was not in the whipping. Or in the paper bags. The pleasure was in going to the Stock Exchange next day and trying to work out which of your colleagues you'd whipped the night before. (*Pause.*) He was funny. I liked him.

CURLY: Jen.

JENNY: He sat in this bar, gin dripping from his chin, from his eyes, gin in the palms of his hands, talking about England. And the need to be whipped. His liver, at the end, was a little orange thing.

CURLY: Who found him?

JENNY: I sent for the police.

CURLY: Does the note explain, say anything, to do with Sarah? The disappearance.

JENNY: It depressed him. He says that.

CURLY: But . . .

JENNY: But he knew nothing concrete. He'd told me that when he was alive. The note's mostly about my getting the club. He'd only bought it originally so that I could manage it. I was out of a job. So he set me up. A bauble.

CURLY: What did you do in return?

JENNY: I did nothing. He was never my lover. It was Sarah he had. (*Pause.*) Getting Sarah to sleep with you. I don't know. I imagine rather a squalid operation. Some nights you could have gathered her up off the floor, and arranged the limbs how you wanted them. She was mad about him. He spilt a whole bottle of gin all over her. She never washed for weeks. Sentimental.

CURLY: What . . .

JENNY: (*At once*) If you shut up I'll tell you. (*Pause.*) She thought
he was like Patrick. Only human. She was obsessed with
her father because he was so complete. Sarah used to say he
had a personality like a pebble. There was no way in. Then
she met Malloy. A man from her father's world. From her
father's class. Of her father's age. A man like her father.
But able to be agonized. Capable of guilt. She was
enthralled.

CURLY: How long did it last?

JENNY: Few weeks.

CURLY: Then . . .

JENNY: There was a row. A few months ago.

CURLY: What about?

CURLY: Sarah said it was about the whipping. That she'd just
found out.

CURLY: Did you believe her?

JENNY: No—the whipping would have been an added attraction.
Another weakness. She'd have loved him more.

CURLY: Then she lied.

JENNY: Sarah never lied. She said people should know
everything.

(*Pause.*)

CURLY: Have you ever met my father?

JENNY: Yes.

CURLY: Have you seen inside the City of London? Inside the
banks and the counting houses? It's perfect. Men with
silver hair and suits with velvet pockets. Oiling down
padded corridors. All their worries papered over with £10
notes and brilliantine. I first went there when I was seven.
The crystal city. You could just hear the money being
raked in like autumn leaves. My father moved as silkily as
anyone. A clear leather desk in a book-lined room. A
golden inkwell. That was all. That and the sound of money
gathering like moss on the side of a wet building. When he
got home at night, out with the cello and the Thackeray.
He made his money with silent indolence. Part of a club. In
theory a speculator. But whoever heard of an English

speculator who actually speculated and lost? Once you
were in, you had it sewn up from paddock to post. Sarah
would know what I'm talking about.

JENNY: The two of you.

CURLY: So I chose guns. The noisiest profession I could find. I
used to set up a client's demonstration of the AR10. You
fire tracer bullets at tin cans filled with gasoline. Did you
ever see a tracer bullet hit a bean can full of petrol? It's
better than a John Wayne movie. The oohs and ahs. I used
to saddle up and ride into the sunset leaving the range a
smouldering ruin. We sold a hell of a lot of guns. Poor
Sarah. I just know what she felt.
(*'Blanket of Blue' is played off, Lomax-style.*)
Let me smell your Scotch.
(*He smiles into the Scotch, then sniffs.*) Did anyone—love
Sarah?

JENNY: Bum business. Look what I got out of it. The Michael
Lomax trio scraping their balls off in an upstairs room.
Dipso . . .
(*Pause.*)

CURLY: Tell me who killed her?

JENNY: It would only have needed the barest suggestion. Sarah,
just put your head under the water. Moving from grey to
grey. She'd have done it. If you asked her. She would have
covered herself in kerosene and set light to it. To win your
affection. (*Pause.*) How Malloy could have touched her.

CURLY: Know what Bernie said?

JENNY: Bernie?

CURLY: Bernie Cornfeld said to me: 'Humanity's a nasty racket
to be in.' (*Pause.*) Miss Wilbur. You see, I even know your
second name. I know everything I have been able to find
out. A little obscure. I know all about your
great-great-grandfather, the Armenian Jew who fucked his
way through the nineteenth century like an Alka-Seltzer. I
know it all since you came over here at fourteen. And I
know dwelling-place, size of flat, name of dog, even dog's
diet, even dog's distaste for Lassie meaty chunks. (*Pause.*)

I'm propositioning you. (*Pause.*) You'd be the first for some time. For some years. The first in fact since the Sheikh of Mina Said's daughter. She went with an arms deal. A little Arab stardust might rub off.

JENNY: What about Malloy?

CURLY: Laying Malloy aside. That's a very nice leg.

JENNY: I've got another one just like it. What about Sarah?

CURLY: Laying Sarah aside. Listen, my dear . . .

JENNY: What do you get out of it?

CURLY: Hopefully some change from a pound.

JENNY: Listen—punk-face—I wouldn't buy what you've got if it was on refrigerated display.

CURLY: I don't suppose I'd be selling under those conditions. (*Pause.*) You come with me.

JENNY: Me Jane.

CURLY: I'll show you the world.

JENNY: Take me to Eastbourne then. Tonight.

CURLY: It's late.

JENNY: Don't you want to go?

CURLY: Go some time.

JENNY: About how you were the best man for the job.

CURLY: All right. I'll get Pat's car.

JENNY: I'll get a wrap.

(*She laughs and moves to go.*)

Lassie meaty chunks.

(JENNY *exits.*)

CURLY: I was once stranded in Alaska for ten days with a single copy of G. E. Moore's *Principia Ethica*. And one copy of *My Gun Is Quick*. The work of Micky Spillane. I was able in this period to make comparisons under scientific test conditions. The longest word in *Principia Ethica* is 'contrahydrapallotistic'. The longest word in Spillane is 'balloon'. Moore wins outright on length of sentence, number of words and ability to contradict yourself in the shortest space. Spillane won on one count only. It burns quicker.

(CURLY *exits.*)

Scene 7

The Delafields' drawing-room. Night.

    MRS DUNNING *is crocheting,* PATRICK *reading. Peace.* PATRICK *looks up, holds his look.* MRS DUNNING *looks across at him. They smile slightly.* PATRICK *goes back to his book, sighs, puts it aside, gets up, sighs again.*

PATRICK: Mrs Dunning.

    (MRS DUNNING *smiles again, does not look up. He stands near her, does not touch her. She smiles at the crochet.*)

MRS DUNNING: I love it when you call me that.

PATRICK: Hold on.

    (PATRICK *loosens his tie, then goes out by the side door.* MRS DUNNING *puts her crochet aside, kicks off her shoes, then pulls off the jumper she is wearing and folds it on the sofa. She takes off her skirt, folds that, then drops a string of pearls into a little heap on the table. She stands in a bra, pants, stockings and suspenders. She gapes a moment. Pause.*)

MRS DUNNING: (*Quietly*) Pat.

    (*She listens for an answer, then goes back to the sofa, picks up her crochet, and continues to work. Pause.* CURLY *comes in from the main door, sees her, looks at his feet.* MRS DUNNING *sees him and half-smiles. He looks at her.* PATRICK *comes in by the side entrance, wearing only trousers and socks. He stops when he sees* CURLY. *Pause.*)

CURLY: I called in on the police.

PATRICK: Ah.

CURLY: No news of Sarah. I want to borrow the car.

    (PATRICK *takes the car keys out of his pocket and throws them lightly across the room.* CURLY *catches the keys and goes out. Pause.* PATRICK *stares a moment, then walks up and down. Pause.*)

PATRICK: Put your clothes on.

    (*He moves to go out.* MRS DUNNING *turns away.*)

    (*Before the start of the next scene the sound of the sea is heard.*)

SCENE 8

The Crumbles. Night.
  *The curtain rises on a bare stage. At once, from down stage, soaking
wet,* JENNY *comes running on, wearing a bathing-costume.*

JENNY: Hallelujah.
    (CURLY *runs on, also fresh from the sea, also in a bathing-costume.*)
CURLY: Hallelujah.
    (CURLY *cartwheels twice.* JENNY *does a handstand over.* CURLY
    *turns her round in a wheel, then she runs towards his out-held hands.
    She steps up and onto his shoulders. They stand in this position,
    looking out into the audience, as still as possible.*)
JENNY: Right.
CURLY: So this is it.
JENNY: The Crumbles.
CURLY: Christ.
JENNY: It's strange. (*Pause.*) It's cold.
CURLY: Cold for September.
JENNY: Cold for one o'clock in the morning.
CURLY: What do you see?
JENNY: (*With relish*) I see suffering and pain and men not happy
    with their lot . . .
CURLY: Do you?
JENNY: I do. I see heavy scowls and fists raised in anger, and I
    see tears of sorrow and of indignation. I see men with axes
    in their backs, acid steaming off their skins, needles in their
    eyeballs, tripping on barbed wire, falling on broken bottles.
    That's what I see.
CURLY: Ah, Eastbourne. Quite unchanged.
JENNY: I see the living dead.
CURLY: What do you see that's nice?
JENNY: Nice?
CURLY: Yeah. You know. Nice.

JENNY: I see men—born happy. It just doesn't show. Let me down.

(*She climbs down from* CURLY*'s shoulders.*)

I'm going to get dressed.

CURLY: Stay.

JENNY: Why?

CURLY: Sit.

(CURLY *sits cross-legged.* JENNY *watches.*)

The colder you get the more you will enjoy being warm.

JENNY: Oh yeah?

CURLY: The essence of pleasure is self-denial.

(CURLY *puts a tattered paper bag on his head.* JENNY *just watches.*)

I come to England maybe once a year. It's a shabby little island, delighted with itself. A few months ago I decided to return.

JENNY: Where's the whip?

CURLY: I was ready for England. I was attracted by news of the property racket. Slapping people on top of people like layers of lasagne. Think about what I'm saying. Don't think about the cold.

JENNY: Forget the cold. Listen to Curly.

CURLY: When I got back I found this country was a jampot for swindlers and cons and racketeers. Not just property.

(JENNY *goes out.*)

(*Unaware that she has gone*) Boarding-houses and bordellos and nightclubs and crooked charter flights, private clinics, horse-hair wigs and tin-can motor cars, venereal cafés with ice-cream made from whale blubber and sausages full of sawdust.

JENNY: (*Off*) Forget the cold. Listen to Curly.

CURLY: Money can be harvested like rotten fruit. People are aching to be fleeced. But those of us who do it must learn the quality of self-control.

(JENNY *reappears with duffle coat and sweater. She looks warm. She is carrying* CURLY*'s clothes.*)

JENNY: Curly, is that why you came back?

CURLY: Wherever I've travelled, wherever I've been, there's

been a tiny echo in my mind. The noise in my father's
office. The slight squelch of Dad's hands in the meat.

JENNY: Why did you come back?

(*She drops his towel near him.* CURLY *takes his bag off.*)

CURLY: I came back because I'm ready. I've grown up.

(*Pause.*)

JENNY: What about Sarah?

CURLY: Sarah. (*Pause.*) Yes, well. That as well.

(*Pause. He wraps himself in his towel.*)

When I went to get the car my father was with Mrs
Dunning. I even detected a moment of shame. He's getting
old. The first crack in the pebble. It made me sad. You
should see her thighs. Like putting your hand between two
slices of liver.

JENNY: You horrible little man. (*Pause.*) Sarah was wide open.
An ever-open wound. Her face was so—open, it just begged
to be kicked. You had to put the boot in. It's . . .

CURLY: All right . . .

JENNY: She was so naive. She used to tell Patrick your wealth is
built on the suffering of the poor. And she expected an
answer.

CURLY: All right.

JENNY: (*Screaming*) All right.

(*She throws his clothes to the ground.*)

Always ready with an innocent question. Why don't you
share what you've got? Why can't people run their own
lives? Why persist with a system you know to be wrong?
How can you bear to be rich when so many people are
poor?

CURLY: Did she say that?

JENNY: Well, what did she expect? (*Pause.*) Christ Jesus. Doesn't
she know there's a war on? She was asking for it.

CURLY: Do you know what Bernie said?

(*Pause.*)

JENNY: No.

CURLY: Bernie Cornfeld said to me: 'Curly,' he said, 'there's
nothing in this world so lovely it can't be shat on.'

JENNY: Right.

CURLY: Right.

JENNY: And this is where she died. (*She yells into the night air.*) Return John Bloom to your kingdom. Jack Cotton, arise from your grave. Harry Hyams, claim your children. (*Pause.*)

CURLY: You know your way around.
   (*He sits on the ground.*)

JENNY: (*She sits.*) I know them all. Their names. And I wonder about . . .

CURLY: (*Smiling*) The state of their souls.

JENNY: (*Smiling*) All right.
   (*Pause.*)

CURLY: I called in on the police when I was getting the car. The railway tickets were first-class. (*Pause.*) Can you imagine . . .

JENNY: Sarah?

CURLY: First . . .

JENNY: Never. (*Pause.*) God. (*Pause.*) Have you spoken to him?

CURLY: Couldn't. (*Pause.*) Look at the night.

JENNY: Yeah.

CURLY: Just look at the water.

JENNY: You don't want to be like them, Curly.
   (CURLY *smiles thinly.*)
   Do you? (*Pause.*) It's such a beautiful night. Isn't it lovely?

CURLY: This is the loveliest it gets.
   (*He gets up and smiles.*)
   I'll take you home. You look wonderful.

JENNY: Curly.

CURLY: Old bean.

JENNY: Is that what you say?

CURLY: What?

JENNY: Is that what you say to a girl you want? 'Old bean'?

CURLY: Sure.

JENNY: I see.

CURLY: Well . . . (*Pause.*) Let's go.

JENNY: Curly.

CURLY: What?

JENNY: First-class.

CURLY: Yes, I know. (*Pause.*) It could have been Malloy.

JENNY: No. Not his—manner. He would never. Especially with her. She wouldn't allow him.

CURLY: So.

JENNY: So.

CURLY: I've thought of nothing else.

JENNY: Why didn't you ask him?

CURLY: I will.

JENNY: Are you afraid? (*Pause.*) That's what I asked you. When we first met.

CURLY: This place gives me the creeps. (*Pause.*) Let's go.

JENNY: The essence of pleasure is self-denial.

(*She rises, picks up all his clothes and his car keys, and taunts him.*)

CURLY: Oh, Jenny, come on.

JENNY: So.

CURLY: For Christ's sake.

(*She throws the keys up in the air as a taunt and catches them herself.*)

JENNY: Wrap up warm.

(*She heads out fast.*)

CURLY: Christ.

(JENNY *goes out with the keys and clothes.*)

JENNY: (*As she goes*) Forget the cold. Listen to Curly . . .

CURLY: (*Bellowing after her*) Patrick's not the only man who travels first-class. (*Pause. Bellowing*) Christ. (*Pause.*) Christ. (*Pause. Muttering*) Christ. (*Pause.*) Control yourself. (*Pause.*) Control. (*Pause.*) I am a pebble. With self-control. (*Pause. He drops the towel at his feet. The lights fade to a spot on* CURLY.)

Eastbourne is a grey city. The lights shine less bright than in LA. I wanted to be on the Santa Monica freeway stopping over at Sloppy Joes for pastrami on rye and one cheese and tomato Anita Ek-burger. I wanted to be in Caracas paying $25 for a Venezuelan sauna. I wanted to be in the Persian mountains playing poker with Kurd guerillas

for lumps of hashish as big as a man's brain. I wanted
to be in that bar in Laos watching that old inverted
sphincter puffing and inhaling, puffing and exhaling: a last
inverted monument to human ingenuity that not even the
Americans could bomb into submission.

(*The lights fade and music swells up, 'We'll Gather Lilacs'—not
the thin Lomax version, the full-bodied BBC Concert Orchestra—as
the curtain falls.*)

PART II

SCENE 9

A Police Station. Day.
Apart from a single flat or cut-out to indicate the setting, the stage is bare
except for the chair on which JENNY is sitting. A POLICEMAN stands by her.

POLICEMAN: Spring of 1924—April twelfth—a man called Patrick
Mahon, lived in London, went to an ironmongers, bought a
meat saw and a 10-inch knife. He then went to Waterloo
station, collected his suitcase and then took a train to
Eastbourne. Waiting in Eastbourne, a Miss Emily Kaye. A
young stenographer he had met in London. The idea was to
rent a small cottage on the beach to conduct what Mahon
referred to as 'a love experiment'. Miss Kaye had prepared
for the experiment by selling some bonds she owned and
giving them to Mr Mahon. The cottage they rented was on
the stretch of beach known as the Crumbles. They moved
in. The experiment lasted three days. On the following
Tuesday, Mahon strangled her and dismembered her body.
He packed some pieces tightly into old boxes and filled
biscuit tins with her innards. He attempted to boil down
her fat in open saucepans. In the middle of the night, in
savage weather, with thunder crashing outside he placed
her severed head on the fire. The intense heat of the flames
caused the eyes of the dead woman to open. Mahon, a 33-
year-old soda fountain salesman, ran from the house. For
the first time, horrified. He returned to London. Later he
was arrested and executed. (*Pause.*) Would anyone in the
family have heard that story before?
JENNY: Well—Patrick's the most highly educated.
   (*A single cello plays.*)

60

SCENE 10

The Hospital Grounds. Day.
    MAX *is discovered, in black, his hands in his pockets.* CURLY *appears,*
    in quite a big overcoat.

CURLY: Glad you could make it. How was the funeral, Max?

MAX: Subdued.

CURLY: Anyone there?

MAX: Just Malloy's mother.

CURLY: No one else?

MAX: And Jenny.

CURLY: And Jenny—ah.

MAX: Yes.

CURLY: How was that?

MAX: What?

CURLY: In black. Did that give you any kind of buzz?

MAX: Listen . . .

CURLY: Uh. Ignore it. Proceed. I'd like to hear your alibi for the
    night Sarah disappeared.

MAX: It's dull.

CURLY: I'm sure it's dull. That's not the point.

MAX: That's a terrible cold you've got.

CURLY: Now you mention it, yes. I got left out on the beach, you
    see. Reconstructing the crime. Alibi.

MAX: I spent the evening with a man called Hart. H-a-r-t. A
    vet. Well, not a vet exactly. Michael Hart is a spiritualist.
    He claims that through animals we may talk to the other
    side.

CURLY: Go on.

MAX: The dead. Animals have a psychic flair for communicating
    with the dead.

CURLY: I see. So your alibi can be confirmed by a reliable dog.

MAX: No. No. Confirmed by your father. It was at his house.

CURLY: Yes?

MAX: You should talk to him.

(CURLY *just stares at him.*)

It was Sarah's idea. I was working on a series about modern religions. Also Sarah's idea. She loved shopping around. She suggested taking Hart and his famous Alsatian to Patrick's. The idea was she would come with me. I just wanted to get her in the same room as her father. But she funked out—so—I was left with Mr Delafield. He wanted to communicate with his dead wife—your mother. I thought the whole thing was in very bad taste. Patrick was quite serious throughout. Hart's Alsatian kept snarling at him—then fell asleep. Without Sarah the whole exercise was hollow.

CURLY: She knew you were both there?

MAX: Oh, yes. She pushed us into it.

CURLY: And she went off to Eastbourne meanwhile?

MAX: We later found out. Yes.

CURLY: Did it occur to you afterwards she could have planned suicide all along and set you two up as a final gag?

MAX: Yes.

CURLY: Rather an elaborate gag.

MAX: Yes.

CURLY: Muttering away at an Alsatian.

MAX: But typical.

CURLY: From what you say.

MAX: Typical of her.

CURLY: No longer a nut case?

(MAX *smiles. Pause.*)

MAX: Check with your father, eh?

CURLY: Yaar. (*Pause.*) As Brigadier-General Bolivar Vallarino of Panama said to me: 'Put it there, pal.'

(*They shake hands. Salute.*)

MAX: What's it to be? Tomorrow—same time, same place?

CURLY: I don't think so, I don't think I want to see you again, Max. Something of the magic has died.

MAX: Well, well.

(CURLY *heads out.*)

Abandoning the investigation?

CURLY: (*Turning back*) Thinking about it.

MAX: That's what your father said you'd do.

CURLY: Did he say that?

MAX: He said being back in England made you want a nice job.

CURLY: I'm looking for an opening certainly.

MAX: I don't know what arms salesmen usually move on to.

CURLY: Allied Professions. The Church, you know, the Law.

(*He waves.*)

MAX: See you some day.

CURLY: Not if I see you first.

(*He sings.*)

Keep young and beautiful
It's your duty to be beautiful
Keep young and beautiful
If you want to be loved.

(*The lights fade to black-out.*)

SCENE 11

The Shadow of the Moon bar. Night.

In the darkness, MAX *follows on immediately with Curly's song from the previous scene.*

MAX:　Keep young and beautiful
It's your duty to be beautiful
Keep young and beautiful
If you want to be loved.

(*The lights come up on the bar scene.* JENNY *is discovered behind the bar. She turns as she hears the singing.* MAX *dances on.*)

JENNY: I thought you were Curly.

MAX: What I say is: the world is a rice pudding. It's just waiting to be skinned.

JENNY: You've met him too?

MAX: Oh yes. My dear.

JENNY: The bar's closed.

MAX: Nice place. Where's the people?

JENNY: Gone home.

MAX: Scotch.

JENNY: Max. You look funny without her.

MAX: I feel funny. No longer the parrot on the shoulder. I get through whole sentences without interruption.

JENNY: I warned you . . .

MAX: What?

JENNY: That she'd kill herself.

MAX: Oh that.

JENNY: That.

(*Pause.*)

MAX: Scotch.

JENNY: I think she said, Max, I'm going to kill myself. And you said just show me. And she did. (*Pause.*) How many times did I tell you?

MAX: Often. You leapt at the opportunity.

JENNY: I was pointing out . . .

MAX: You did best all round.

JENNY: What do you mean?

MAX: This place. You win the Shadow of the Moon.

(*Pause.*)

JENNY: I see.

MAX: Well, so you're happy.

JENNY: Max.

MAX: Now the lover is buried.

JENNY: He was not my lover.

MAX: He just left you the club.

JENNY: It was nothing to do with it.

MAX: Tell that to Mrs Malloy.

JENNY: Malloy married . . .

JENNY: Malloy's mother. At the funeral. Mrs Malloy.

(*Pause.*)

JENNY: What are you talking about?

MAX: I have a photo of you in a gymslip.

64

(*He steps behind the bar to* JENNY.) With a straw hat and black
socks.

JENNY: What about Mrs Malloy?

MAX: This is a knife. Kiss me. (*Pause.*) Hands behind head.
(*She does so.*)
Now follow me out from behind the bar.
(*They come out. We see the knife.*)
Sit down. Keep your hands there.
(*She sits down. He sits opposite.*)
I sit myself down. Don't move.
(*The knife is held by* MAX *for the scene.*)
There aren't many girls left in Guildford.

JENNY: No.

MAX: Speak up.

JENNY: I said no, not many.

MAX: What with Juliet. And Fizz and Laura gone now. And the
other Laura. And Jane Hammond got passed down the
line. And the one with the lisp. They tell me Alice has been
had by most of the Bank of England . . .

JENNY: So I hear.

MAX: Sally and Pip . . .

JENNY: Yes . . .

MAX: Both to chartered accountants, inevitably. Gloria, married.
Janice. I'm scraping the very bottom of the barrel. Tamara.
That doesn't leave many. Any. Of the ones who used to
come here. And the ones who didn't come here were
rubbish. Sarah would do anything you wanted. (*Pause.*)
Rather a disgusting characteristic. (*Pause.*) Penny on her
seventh actor and Jacqueline a nun. That leaves you. Oh,
Jenny. What happens to people?

JENNY: I don't know.

MAX: When we came here as teenagers—you and me and
Sarah—you never knew what would happen. It seemed the
most ambiguous place in the world. Like falling into satin
in the dark. And look at it now. (*Pause.*) Tell me what you
think of Curly. (*Pause.*) You know he's given up looking for
Sarah already.

JENNY: I didn't know that.

MAX: He's everything the world wasn't going to be. Blustering. And sneering. And insincere. Is that really what you want?

JENNY: Then put the knife away.

MAX: Do you really want Curly?

JENNY: He's never touched me, Max. (*Pause.*) Tell me about Mrs Malloy.

MAX: Do you really know nothing? (*Pause.*) She's in hospital. She may not have been mad when she went in. But she's certainly mad now. Jennifer. (*Pause.*) I find your innocence unforgivable. (*Pause.*) Take off your clothes.
(*Nothing.*)
Lie down on the floor.
(*Nothing.*)
Close your eyes, open your mouth, praise the Lord and thank God you're British. (*Pause.*) Goodnight.
(MAX *goes out immediately, putting the knife away. The lights change.*)

JENNY: Young women in Guildford must expect to be threatened. Men here lead ugly lives and girls are the only touchstones left. Cars cruise beside you as you walk down the pavement, I have twice been attacked at the country club, the man in the house opposite has a telephoto lens, my breasts are often touched on commuter trains, my body is covered with random thumbprints, the doctor says he needs to undress me completely to vaccinate my arm, men often spill drinks in my lap, or brush cigarettes against my bottom, very old men bump into me and clutch at my legs as they fall. I have been offered drinks, money, social advancement and once an editorial position on the *Financial Times*. I expect this to go on. I expect to be bumped, bruised, followed, assaulted, stared at and propositioned for the rest of my life, while at the same time offering sanctuary, purity, reassurance, prestige—the only point of loveliness in men's ever-darkening lives.

Scene 12

Guildford Railway Station. Night.

    JENNY *is sitting on a bench reading a newspaper. A* PORTER *and* CURLY *enter from opposite sides.* CURLY *has a briefcase and umbrella.*

JENNY: Well. You're getting very hard to find.

CURLY: Get my luggage, will you? And a taxi.

PORTER: Sir.

    (*The* PORTER *goes out.*)

JENNY: (*Allowing nothing*) They tell me your heart's gone out of it. The investigation.

CURLY: Can't do it all the time.

JENNY: Even thinking of a job. Insurance. Something like Lloyd's.

CURLY: Well, I've been up to town. Just to talk it over.

JENNY: Costs a lot of money.

CURLY: Seventy-five thousand entrance fee. That's all a chap needs. Buy himself a slice of security.

JENNY: (*Lethally*) I brought you the keys to your car.

    (JENNY *throws the keys over.* CURLY *catches them, embarrassed.*)

    Little man.

CURLY: (*Smiling*) Jenny.

JENNY: And some information. (*Pause.*) I've been to see a Mrs Malloy. She's 73. Initials E. R. Malloy. As, she said, like the Queen. Am I keeping you?

CURLY: No, no.

JENNY: Malloy's mother lived in one house for the whole of her life. A Victorian house in the centre of Guildford. Married for a month in 1918 before her husband was killed at Chemin des Dames. At the age of 68 she transferred the house into her son's name. Tax dodge: you avoid death duties. Standard practice round here. She put it in her son's name. But she went on living there herself. So. Central

Guildford. Torn apart as you know. And some develop-
ers bought the rest of the block. It tempted Malloy. He held
the deeds. There was only one obstacle. His mother had
lived there the whole of her life. He held out for a couple of
months. Then suddenly cracked. He had her committed.

CURLY: Was she mad?

JENNY: Oh, Curly, come on.

CURLY: Was she mad?

JENNY: She was mad when enough people needed her to be.
Let's face it. She was pushed. Malloy signed the committal
order.

CURLY: Is there any actual evidence she was pushed?

JENNY: Oh, Curly . . .

CURLY: How much did he make?

JENNY: Two hundred thousand.

(*Pause.*)

CURLY: She was pushed.

JENNY: (*Rising*) And another property thrown in. A run-down
old barn on the other side of town. A nightclub called the
Shadow of the Moon. Mrs Malloy in the mental hospital
sent her nurse on an errand. The nurse was Sarah. Where
the old woman's house had been she found seventeen floors
of prestige offices crowned with an antique supermarket.
She went back to the hospital. Everyone should know
everything. That's what she said. She told the old woman
her house had gone. If she wasn't mad before, she certainly
is now. (*Pause.*) Sarah was electrified when she found out.
No wonder she rowed with Malloy. Can you imagine? Her
friend Malloy—one of life's losers turns out to be a shark.
She would have flipped. She would have told everyone. But
the amazing thing is: she didn't. For the first time in her life
she kept something secret. From me, from everyone. Except
Max. Max was a journalist. He would have said what a
wonderful story. Stockbroker Swindles His Own Mother in
Property Deal. But the story never appeared. I think he
went to Malloy and blackmailed him. (*Pause.*) Do you want
to go back to London?

CURLY: How do you know all this?

JENNY: Partly from Max.

CURLY: Did he tell you?

JENNY: He . . .

CURLY: What?

JENNY: Signalled he knew.

CURLY: How?

JENNY: With a knife. He came to the club last night. He thought I knew.

CURLY: What made him think that?

JENNY: Because Malloy was in love with me, that's why he left the Shadow of the Moon to me. Max thought it was because Malloy was my lover.

CURLY: Whereas in fact . . .

JENNY: It was because he was never my lover.

CURLY: Yes. That makes perfect sense round here. So if Max did blackmail Malloy, you're saying he only had one problem . . .

JENNY: The old problem we have met before.

CURLY: How to close Sarah's mouth.

JENNY: Sarah will want to know why Max hasn't published the story.

CURLY: God . . .

JENNY: How to shut her up . . .

CURLY: What a beautiful girl this Sarah is. Niagara. Vesuvius. Grinding on against injustice and the misery of the world.

JENNY: Max's only problem . . .

CURLY: Yaaar.

(*Pause.*)

JENNY: Is that what happened?

CURLY: Why take her to the Crumbles?

JENNY: Because in 1924 there was a particularly disgusting murder there.

CURLY: Well, exactly.

JENNY: What?

CURLY: Why draw attention to yourself? The Crumbles. The worst possible place. It's the Wembley Stadium of murder already.

JENNY: (*Quietly*) Right.

(*Pause.* CURLY *turns and looks at her. Dead quiet, please.*)

CURLY: What do you mean he had a knife?

JENNY: I've just said it.

CURLY: Tell me.

(JENNY *shakes her head.*)

What happened?

JENNY: Why should I?

CURLY: Jenny.

JENNY: He never came near.

CURLY: Jenny. (*Pause.*) I'm not telling you the truth.

JENNY: I wouldn't expect it.

CURLY: I don't like to be honest. It's not in my nature.

JENNY: (*Smiling*) Go on.

CURLY: I'd heard a bit about Malloy, not about his mother, that surprises me, but about his house. You see, on a crooked deal a blackmailer will have a choice of targets. Malloy. Or the property company. Or the man who finances the property company. That old Victorian house? Patrick's money bought it.

(*Pause.*)

JENNY: Max blackmails Patrick . . .

CURLY: Congratulations.

JENNY: Max gets rid of Sarah, then forces Patrick into confirming his ludicrous alibi about the dog.

CURLY: You're very quick. (*Pause.*) They seem to have lost my luggage.

JENNY: Which one will you go for first?

CURLY: You're very keen.

JENNY: You getting frightened, Curly? Is that what it is? Losing your nerve? Frightened to hurt your father? Frightened to face up to him?

CURLY: Face up to Spats.

JENNY: What luggage?

CURLY: All my things. I'm moving down here. Get a job. Get a house. I like the atmosphere. (*Pause.*) Don't stare at me, kid. (*Pause.*) Listen, the story's ridiculous. It's full of holes. If Max went to blackmail my father, he would have just said he didn't know.

JENNY: But for the property company conning an old woman is bad publicity.

CURLY: It happens all the time. It's called business practice, people go to the wall.

JENNY: Nobody would believe them.

CURLY: They'd say they didn't know. It's just a matter of keeping your nerve and a plausible story.

JENNY: Who's to say it's plausible?

CURLY: Exactly. Newspapers can be bought, judges can be leant on, politicians can be stuffed with truffles and cognac. Life's a racket, that we know.

JENNY: Christ, I'll make a person of you yet.

CURLY: Forget it. (*Pause.*) Listen—sugar plum—the horror of the world. The horror of the world is there are no excuses left. There was a time when men who ruined other men, could claim they were ignorant or simple or believed in God, or life was very hard, or we didn't know what we were doing, but now everybody knows the tricks, the same shabby hands have been played over and over, and men who persist in old ways of running their countries or their lives, those men now do it in the full knowledge of what they're doing. So that at last greed and selfishness and cruelty stand exposed in white neon: men are bad because they want to be. No excuses left.

JENNY: You mean you're not going to see him?

CURLY: (*Smiling*) No, I'm not.

JENNY: Well, why not just say that? (*Pause.*) Like to have known you better, Curly.

(*The* PORTER *wheels on* CURLY's *luggage, a huge Singapore trunk.* JENNY *goes out.*)

PORTER: Here she is, sir. (*Pause.*) Moving down here, are you, sir?

CURLY: No. Change of plan. Left luggage. Twenty-four hours.

(CURLY *heads off. 'We'll Gather Lilacs' is heard, Lomax-style.*)

Scene 13

The Shadow of the Moon bar. Night.
The BARMAN *is alone behind his bar.* CURLY *walks in, vicious, drunk and smoking.*

CURLY: Give me a scotch.
BARMAN: Right away, sir.
CURLY: And don't be so bloody pleasant.
BARMAN: Sir.
CURLY: Now go upstairs, knock politely on her door and tell her there's something slimy to see her.
(*He takes the bottle and glass.*)
BARMAN: Sir.
(*The* BARMAN *goes out.*)
CURLY: (*Shouting*) For God's sake, Lomax, give us all a break. Just shut up.
(*'We'll Gather Lilacs' stumbles and stops.*)
(*Sitting at the table*) Not as if anyone was dancing up there. Just looks like the bloody *Titanic*.
(*The* BARMAN *returns.*)
BARMAN: She says . . .
CURLY: Yes, Barman?
BARMAN: She says, 'Piss off.' Sir.
CURLY: White-knickered do-good cock-shrivelling cow.
BARMAN: She wants you to go, sir.
CURLY: Want to make something of it, Barman?
(*He threatens the* BARMAN *with the bottle.*)
BARMAN: Sir.
CURLY: I'm glad I didn't sell you a gun.
JENNY: (*Off*) Mike. Get scraping.
(CURLY *turns at the strips.*)
CURLY: Down I go.
(CURLY *exits.*)

LOMAX: (*Off*) Come on, everybody. Let's bossa nova.
(*The Lomax Band plays a bossa nova.*)

SCENE 14

The Hospital Grounds. Night.
 MAX *is tapping his knife, unopened, against his hand. After a moment* CURLY *appears, in a big overcoat.*

CURLY: Hullo, Max.

MAX: Hullo.

CURLY: I'm sorry to drag you out here in the middle of the night.

MAX: That's all right.

CURLY: At barely ten minutes' notice.

MAX: That's all right.

CURLY: No, it's not. You should be angry. (*Pause.*) You're an
    innocent party. Act angry. (*Pause.*) Story is you murdered
    Sarah. We don't believe that, do we, Max? We don't think
    you're the murdering type.
    (MAX *flashes his flick-knife out.*)
    (*Quickly taking out his gun*) Every man has his own gun.
    That's not a metaphor. That's a fact. Only some have more
    guns than others. Knife.
    (MAX *hands his knife to* CURLY.)
    I have a bottle in my pocket. Remove it.
    (MAX *tenderly takes the bottle from* CURLY's *pocket.*)
    And put it down there.
    (MAX *puts it on the ground.*)
    And stay down. (*Hard and fast*) I think you took money,
    Max. That was your crime. It's not the local custom, I
    have observed. In England they don't take money. They
    make money. Spot the difference. It's a country of
    opportunity. Everyone can run a racket of their own. Say I
    discover some property developers have used unusual
    pressures to achieve their aims. I don't go and ask for a

share of their money. I go out and find a defenceless old
cow of my own to swindle. That is the creative thing to do.

MAX: I'd never taken money before.

CURLY: I don't care. Your back is snapped. From now till the
millennium. They have your number. (*Pause.*) Have a drink.

MAX: No, thank you.

CURLY: Have a drink.

> (MAX *takes a swig.*)
>
> I don't think you have it in you to kill. But, Christ, you
> have it in you to wheedle. Have another drink.
>
> (MAX *takes a swig.*)
>
> Sarah told you about the deal. You were to investigate. But
> you didn't go to Malloy. You went to Patrick. For cash. I
> have one question. Why did Patrick consent?
>
> (MAX *shrugs.*)
>
> Please don't lie to me, Max. Have another drink.
>
> (MAX *drinks again.*)
>
> Pretend you're Malloy.
>
> (MAX *drinks again.*)
>
> Why did Patrick give you the money?

MAX: He . . .

CURLY: Have another drink.

> (MAX *drinks again.*)
>
> Why did Patrick bother? He should have kept his nerve. He
> had a perfectly plausible story . . .

MAX: He . . .

CURLY: Drink.

> (MAX *drinks again.*)
>
> Have a cigarette.
>
> (CURLY *throws down a cigarette and a box of matches.* MAX *lights
> up.*)
>
> He could have said he never knew. Is that not what people
> say? In such circumstances.

MAX: He . . .

CURLY: Drink.

> (MAX *drinks again.*)
>
> I understand he arranged the bridging loan for the

building. He would barely have been implicated.

MAX: There . . .

CURLY: Drink.

(MAX *drinks again.*)

It's a half-baked sort of scandal that I can't quite understand. That's why I'm asking for your help. Have another cigarette.

(MAX *lights a second cigarette, then lights two for* CURLY. CURLY *sticks one in Max's nose and one in Max's right ear.*)

Drink.

(MAX *drinks, coughs and splutters and drops the cigarettes.*)

You're just about ready to tell me the truth.

MAX: They put a dog in . . .

CURLY: Dog?

MAX: Hart . . .

CURLY: The spiritualist . . .

MAX: Yes. Uses his dogs for other purposes . . .

CURLY: The ones that talk to the dead?

MAX: Can also be hired out on eviction jobs.

CURLY: But Malloy sold up.

MAX: Not at first. He wouldn't be bought. So they decided to flush him out of the house. Mrs Malloy was at the cinema. Malloy was alone. Hart stole the fuses. Then put an Alsatian in.

CURLY: What happened?

MAX: Malloy blew it apart with a shotgun.

CURLY: God almighty.

MAX: He did it in the dark. It was the fight of his life. He knew it was Hart's, he phoned him. I'm going to be sick.

CURLY: Don't—be sick. That means Patrick wasn't there that night. And it wasn't his dog. And it's not even publicly his profit. You had nothing on him. Why did he pay?

MAX: I had something on him. I had Sarah on him. He was terrified she'd find out that he was behind it. He was thinking of Sarah. He paid up. He loved her.

CURLY: Mistake.

MAX: On the last day—Sarah found out. It had been—it had

been . . .

CURLY: Like holding Niagara . . .

MAX: Yes . . .

CURLY: Everyone should know everything.

MAX: Yes.

CURLY: How did she take it?

MAX: She was possessed. She'd killed a dog before.

CURLY: Yes.

MAX: When she was a child.

CURLY: Yes.

MAX: She kept saying: what happens to dogs.

CURLY: What happens to dogs.

MAX: What happens to people.

(*Pause.*)

CURLY: Finish the bottle.

MAX: I . . .

CURLY: Finish.

(MAX *drinks again.* CURLY *makes him finish; then bangs down his fist on the end; then gets up.*)

Now get up.

MAX: I can't.

CURLY: Take your empties. And go.

(MAX *crawls off.* CURLY *stamps out the cigarette ends. The lights change.*)

So it came back to Spats. It would always come back to Spats. The world is not run by innocents or small men who happen to believe the wrong thing. It is run by uncomfortably large, obscenely quiet men called Spats. The time was coming when I'd have to face Patrick. Patrick was no longer perfect. I had found a way in. In the thick, densely carpeted air of a merchant bank, the sound of a slight scuffle and the warm red smell of dog. Glimpsed for a second the implausible face of a man who loved his own daughter. I was in.

(*Music starts.*)

SCENE 15

The Delafields' drawing-room. Night.
  CURLY *is sitting in his overcoat with his feet up, waiting. The door opens and* PATRICK *comes in, bleary-eyed, in dressing-gown and pyjamas.*

PATRICK: Curly.
CURLY: Happy birthday, Spats.
PATRICK: Did you just wake me up?
CURLY: Come in. Sit down.
PATRICK: What's happened?
CURLY: You're OK. Sit down.
       (PATRICK *sits.*)
PATRICK: I'd like a glass of hot water.
CURLY: Not yet.
       (PATRICK *gets his little box out.*)
       Put your eyes in. Attaboy.
       (PATRICK *leans back and dabs contact lenses on to his eyes.*)
       Can you see me now?
PATRICK: Yes.
CURLY: I have my fingers on your throat. Feel anything? There's
       been a development. Stray dog. About a year ago. You
       were avoiding a public enquiry, I should think. Irreparable
       damage to the character of Guildford. So someone decided
       to flush out Malloy.
PATRICK: Well?
CURLY: Well?
PATRICK: I know what you're talking about. And I didn't
       condone their methods. Stupid. I was appalled.
CURLY: You didn't know at the time?
PATRICK: I run a merchant bank. I sanctioned the
       purchase—not the method of purchase.
CURLY: But he brought you the corpse.
PATRICK: The dead dog? Yes. He left it on my doorstep. A

77

tuppenny gesture.

CURLY: How did he know that you were behind it?

PATRICK: He worked in the City. Remember. He could fight his way through. He knew the routes.

CURLY: But why did he sell? After he'd blown the dog apart. It was his victory. Why did he not seize it?

(*Pause.*)

PATRICK: Why do people give in? Because they recognize the way things are. He had made his point. He'd planted his tiny flag on the hillside and now—well, if you saw the site—there was just this old Victorian house, alone among the rubble of a demolition site. You looked at it. It was aching to come down. It had to.

CURLY: I don't understand.

PATRICK: Think. Even after that night, to hold on to the house would have meant turning your life into a battlefield, a constant act of self-assertion. Nobody wants to live like that. Straining endlessly to make your point. And why? He already had the moral victory. I glimpsed his face the following morning on the eight thirty-three. He looked up at me. A pleasurable glow of self-righteousness—the fight of his life and he'd won . . .

CURLY: Weren't you ashamed?

PATRICK: He had the righteousness. I had the house. (*Pause.*) Peace with honour. That is the phrase. It means surrender. But of a very special kind. With the sweet heart of your integrity intact. (*Pause.*) He had that. I had—well, so far it's nudging into its third million . . .

CURLY: This moral victory—the fight of his life . . .

PATRICK: Yes?

CURLY: Wasn't much use in his dying year.

PATRICK: That wasn't my fault. Peace with honour—peace with shame. It's a very thin line. A matter of believing—your own propaganda. (*Pause.*) And all for a girl.

CURLY: Everyone loves Jenny.

(*Pause.*)

PATRICK: Stick to your story I used to say. When I met Malloy

78

later in the street. In the last days of alcoholic
collapse. I told him. Stick to your story. You killed the
dog. You revealed my corruption. Great victory. Old man.
(*Pause.*) Curly. Life is pain. Pure and simple. Pain.
Around. Below. All pain. But we have a choice. Either to
protest noisily—to scream against the pain, to rattle and
wail—or else—to submerge that pain, to channel it . . .
(*Pause.*) Preferably in someone else's direction. (*Pause.*) If I
admitted everything that had happened in my life, laid it
out in a field like the contents of an air disaster, would it
really help?

CURLY: Go back to Sarah.

PATRICK: No.

CURLY: Everyone should know everything? That's what I
believe.

PATRICK: Very well.

CURLY: You went to Max.

PATRICK: Not at all. He came to us. Saying he knew about Mrs
Malloy. We had nothing to fear . . .

CURLY: You'd have kept your nerve.

PATRICK: I should hope so . . .

CURLY: And a plausible story.

PATRICK: He said he knew about the dog. Again it was nothing.
We could have denied all knowledge.

CURLY: In fact you do.

PATRICK: Oh, yes. (*Pause.*) Of course. We sent him away. It
was rubbish. But as an afterthought he said he'd tell
Sarah. (*Pause.*) Curly. You may not believe it. The City of
London once enjoyed a reputation for unimpeachable
integrity. My word is my bond. So fabulously wealthy as
to be almost beyond wealth. But in the last twenty years
we've been dragged through the mud like everyone else.
The wide boys and the profiteers have sullied our
reputation. We work now like stallholders against a
barrage of abuse. (*Pause.*) Who is to set standards? Curly.
Who is to lead? You have to be able to believe—my
daughter should not be given the chance to doubt—we

were honest men . . . (*Pause.*) We are honest men. She
had always abused me. But she had never been able to fault
me. (*Pause.*) I had to buy Dupree. Do you understand? For
her sake.

(CURLY *smiles.*)

CURLY: How did you buy him?

PATRICK: A package. Rather lurid. I got him—a job in London
and a series of leads on my younger, less scrupulous
colleagues, gave him a little money . . .

CURLY: Is that all?

PATRICK: No. We negotiated.

CURLY: What?

PATRICK: A large anonymous donation to an anarchist party of
his own choosing. (*Pause.*) On those terms he could take it.
Do you see?

CURLY: Go on.

PATRICK: That was it.

CURLY: Apart from Sarah.

PATRICK: Apart from Sarah that was it. (*Pause.*) Sarah.
Unquenchable. A deep well of unhappiness down which I
could have thrown anarchist subscriptions, dead dogs, pints
of my own warm blood, I could have turned on my head,
destroyed my own life, and still she would not have been
satisfied. (*Pause.*) Like you. (*Pause.*) The two of you. Like
woodpeckers. Nothing will stop you. In her case it was pity
for the world. In yours . . .

CURLY: Go on.

PATRICK: In yours . . .

CURLY: Go on.

PATRICK: Disgust. (*Pause.*) You have a beady little heart, Curly.
It pumps away. I've watched. One thing fires you. The
need to ensure everyone is as degraded as you are.

(*Pause.*)

CURLY: Go on.

PATRICK: Max was like the rest of us. He got worn down. By the
endless wanting to know. Now she wanted to know why the
story had never appeared. (*Pause.*) He told her. Your father

is financing the building. I have been paid off. Malloy was paid off. A dog is dead. Everyone should know everything. She went mad. (*Pause.*) The dog in particular. She was obsessed with the dog. She went straight to Victoria. I followed as soon as I could. (*Pause.*) I got into Eastbourne at midnight. The last train down. It was too late to try all the hotels. I went down to the promenade. By the silver railings there was a girl in a light-coloured raincoat. She had black frizzy hair. It was dark and drizzling and I couldn't see. She was squatting down. As I got nearer I could see she was pissing. On the promenade. She finished. She got up. And her coat was open. She was wearing nothing underneath. It was raining and it was very cold. She just wandered away. (*Pause.*) That's Eastbourne beach. (*Pause.*) I started to follow her. I had no choice.

CURLY: What did she say?

PATRICK: She said nothing.

CURLY: Go on.

PATRICK: We walked. A procession of two, through acres of bungalows to the open land. A flat rocky patch stretching away to the sea. The distance between us religiously observed. (*Pause.*) She sat down on the concrete jetty. (*Pause.*) Those who wish to reform the world should first know a little bit about it. I told her some stories of life in the City—the casual cruelty of each day; take-over bids, redundancies, men ruined overnight, jobs lost, trusts betrayed, reputations smashed, life in that great trough called the City of London, sploshing about in the cash. And I asked, what I have always asked: how will that ever change?

CURLY: Tell me of any society that has not operated in this way.

PATRICK: Five years after a revolution . . .

CURLY: The shit rises . . .

PATRICK: The same pattern . . .

CURLY: The weak go to the wall . . .

PATRICK: Somebody's bound to get hurt . . .

CURLY: You can't make omelettes . . .

PATRICK: The pursuit of money is a force for progress . . .

CURLY: It's always been the same . . .

PATRICK: The making of money . . .

CURLY: The breaking of men.

PATRICK: The two together. Always. The sound of progress.

CURLY: The making of money. The breaking of men.

(*Pause.*)

PATRICK: If I didn't do it . . .

CURLY: Somebody else would. (*Pause.*) And what did she say?

PATRICK: She said nothing. (*Pause.*) Finally, after twenty-one years she said nothing. Wrapped the mac tighter about her body. (*Pause.*) We watched the dawn. If I'd moved towards the jetty she would have thrown herself in. At five-thirty she was calm. She still said nothing. I took the decision. I walked into the town. I rang Hart from the Cavendish and told him to come and collect her. Then I got a train up to town.

CURLY: What?

PATRICK: I had a meeting. (*Pause.*) Money. (*Pause.*) Hart arrived to look after her at a quarter past seven. He was to drive her back. He followed my instructions to the beach. She was gone. Her raincoat was on the jetty. It was the only article of clothing she'd been wearing. It's safe to say she killed herself. (*Pause.*) The suicide was calculated from the start. Not uncommon. She had challenged Max to make me come to Eastbourne. Two malicious gestures. She had chosen to die at a place famous for a ghastly murder. And second, she had left two first-class tickets behind. The clearest possible way of saying—someone else is involved. (*Pause.*) It was me. (*Pause.*) She had to bang down her flag. Like everyone else.

CURLY: How do I know this is true? (*He rises.*) For all I know, you travelled down with her. You could have killed her.

PATRICK: Is that what you think?

(*Pause.*)

CURLY: No. I believe you absolutely. The story has just the right amount of quiet. She slipped obligingly into the sea. An

English murder. Who needs ropes or guns or daggers?
We can trust our victims to pass quietly in the night. Slip
way into the bottle. Or the looney bin. Just—fall away with
barely the crack of a knuckle as they go. (*Pause.*) I'm sure
she died on the beach. I'm sure that you—were 60 miles
away.

PATRICK: I didn't go to the police. I rigged up the alibi with
Hart and Dupree.

CURLY: You left her to die.

PATRICK: No, that's what the police would have said.

CURLY: That's what you did.

PATRICK: It was a knife-edge decision. In the morning light. To
stay or go. I had to decide which was better. Then
something she said made up my mind for me.

CURLY: She spoke.

PATRICK: Just once.

CURLY: What did she say?

PATRICK: A single thing. 'What I despise most,' she said, 'is your
pretence to be civilized.' (*Pause.*) I was reassured. The same
old propaganda. The noise of someone who's going to live.
The same old drivel. She was bleating again. So I left.

CURLY: In fact . . .

PATRICK: In fact she meant it. (*Pause.*) And that is the nail on
which my life is hung. She meant it. (*Pause.*) But I see no
reason to drag it out in public.

CURLY: Sure . . .

PATRICK: If I wish to continue . . .

CURLY: Making money . . .

PATRICK: The facts must be suppressed. The girl is dead. It
makes no difference now.
(*Pause.*)

CURLY: I possess a lethal combination of facts. Suppose I go to
the press? The old woman, the dog, abandoning your
daughter on the beach . . .

PATRICK: (*Calling*) Mrs Dunning. (*To* CURLY) You let it out. You
ruin me. He left his daughter to kill herself. A despicable
thing to do. Bad publicity. I leave my job. What happens?

Someone else pops up in my place. Life covers up
pretty fast. Only the people bleed. (*Calling*) Mrs Dunning.
(*To* CURLY) Both of you did well. You wrung from me the
sane confession. You wanted me to say I was degraded.
Well . . . (*Pause.*) I am. (*Pause.*) OK? So now can I please
go back to work?

(MRS DUNNING *comes in, also in a dressing-gown.*)

MRS DUNNING: You must be quiet, Pat.

PATRICK: I'm sorry.

MRS DUNNING: You must stay calm. You'd better go to bed.

PATRICK: I'm sorry.

MRS DUNNING: That's all right. You'll be fine.

CURLY: I just want to say . . .

MRS DUNNING: Sssh. Be quiet. Come to bed.

CURLY: Let me say . . .

MRS DUNNING: Sssh. Quiet please. Let's everyone be quiet.
(*Pause.*) All right, Pat?

(*She smiles and kisses* PAT *on the cheek.*)

PATRICK: My darling.

MRS DUNNING: Good night.

PATRICK: Good night.

(PATRICK *goes out.*)

MRS DUNNING: (*At the door*) And we'll try to forget you were ever
disturbed.

(MRS DUNNING *goes out.* CURLY *is left alone. The lights change.*)

CURLY: Under the random surface of events lie steel-grey
explanations. The more unlikely and implausible the facts,
the more rigid the obscene geometry below. I was holding
my father's life in my hands. I had to make up my mind. If
I ditched my father, told the newspapers the story of those
days, all I would be doing would be to bang down my tiny
flag on the same mountain-side as Sarah. Somewhere every
so often in this world there will appear this tiny little weed
called morality. It will push up quietly through the tarmac
and there my father will be waiting with a cement grinder
and a shovel to concrete it over. It is inadequate. It cannot
help us now. There are no excuses left. Two sides. Two

sides only. Lloyd's of London was beckoning me. I
could feel its soft fiscal embrace. I wanted its quiet and its
surety. I would sit in Lloyd's and wait for the end. I lay
back. But I wanted Jenny beside me. I wanted to rest my
head between her legs. I was ready to chase the same
shadow, to tread the same path as Dupree and Malloy: all
of us after the same one thing: the hard, bright, glistening
girl who ran the Shadow of the Moon.
(*Music, 'We'll Gather Lilacs', very loud.*)

SCENE 16

The Shadow of the Moon bar. Night.
    JENNY *is in the bar. As the music stops,* CURLY *enters.*

CURLY: Come for a quick one.
JENNY: Come in.
CURLY: Bet I'm the worse soak you ever had.
    (JENNY *smiles and gets him a bottle.*)
    You're up pretty early.
JENNY: Yes. Do you want some breakfast?
CURLY: I . . .
    (JENNY *looks up.*)
    I talked to Patrick.
JENNY: What did he say?
CURLY: He knew nothing. It turned out.
JENNY: You mean. . . ?
CURLY: He really is completely innocent.
JENNY: What about Malloy?
CURLY: That was—quite another business.
JENNY: I see.
CURLY: Nothing to do with it. Or with Patrick. He didn't know.
JENNY: Why did she kill herself?
CURLY: Well . . . (*Pause.*) You said it. She was paranoid. I think
    she got depressed.

JENNY: Nothing to do with Malloy . . .

CURLY: No.

JENNY: Or Patrick.

CURLY: No.

JENNY: I see.

CURLY: She just wasn't quite cut out for things.

CURLY: No . . .

CURLY: Looking back. Inevitable. You understand.

CURLY: Oh, yes.

(*Pause.*)

CURLY: Some people. You can see it coming.

JENNY: I got a letter this morning. Shall I read it to you?

CURLY: Please.

(JENNY *takes out a sheet, leans against the bar, reads:*)

JENNY: 'My darlings, whoops that fig juice if you're wondering.
Let us rejoice in the ugliness of the world. Strangely, I am not upset. I am reassured. I think I left a finger pointing on the beach.

Jenny, keep Pat on the flat of his back. On his knees. Keep him confessing. Keep the wound fresh.

I walked five miles before I found any clothes.

Insist we are degraded.

Resist all those who tell you otherwise.

At all costs fight innocence.

Forbid ignorance.

Startle your children.

Appal your mothers.

Know everything.

Love everything.

Especially—

Decay.

Insist on decay.

I have twice been debauched in the open road. I am travelling at this moment through France. Don't tell Pat. Goodbye, sweet friends, goodbye.'

(*Pause.*)

I think it's from her. I don't know anyone else . . . (*Pause.*)

He called me up.

CURLY: Who?

JENNY: Patrick.

CURLY: What did he say?

JENNY: He said . . . (*Pause.*) Don't look so worried.

CURLY: (*Smiling*) No, no . . .

JENNY: This was yesterday.

CURLY: Ah.

JENNY: He said he'd like to buy this place.

CURLY: Here?

JENNY: Yeah.

CURLY: What did you say?

CURLY: He's offering a very good price.

CURLY: I'm sure.

JENNY: It's a crummy sort of building as you can see.

CURLY: Yeah . . .

JENNY: You know . . .

CURLY: Yeah . . .

JENNY: Some whisky stains and a few tears . . .

CURLY: Jenny . . .

JENNY: I said no.

    (*Pause.*)

CURLY: Jenny . . .

JENNY: So . . .

CURLY: Oh, Jenny . . .

    (*Pause.*)

JENNY: Thanks for your help.

CURLY: What?

JENNY: Sarah.

CURLY: Well . . .

JENNY: Thank you. (*Pause.*) I had a long talk with Michael Hart. About Malloy. And the dog. And Patrick's behaviour on the beach. (*Pause.*) I know everything. (*Pause.*) So do you.

    (*Pause.*)

CURLY: Keep your chin up.

JENNY: And you.

CURLY: (*Backing away*) I liked your legs. I've always liked your legs.

JENNY: Goodbye.

CURLY: Goodbye.

(JENNY *goes out. The lights change.*)

Why should I feel ashamed of myself? Why should I feel inferior? Why should I feel anything? Jenny would go to the newspaper. They didn't believe her. And, anyway, Sarah was alive. It was autumn again. In the mean square mile of the City of London they were making money. (*Smiling*) Back to my guns.

(*The lights fade.*)

Licking Hitler

For Reg

Characters

ANNA SEATON

ARCHIE MACLEAN

WILL LANGLEY

JOHN FENNEL

EILEEN GRAHAM

KARL

HERR JUNGKE

ALLARDYCE

LOTTERBY

LORD MINTON

Chauffeur, Maids, Sergeant,
Soldiers, Naval Commander,
Engineers, Officers, Nurse,
Voice of Narrator

Licking Hitler was first shown on BBC TV on 10 January 1978. The cast was as follows:

ANNA SEATON	Kate Nelligan
ARCHIE MACLEAN	Bill Paterson
WILL LANGLEY	Hugh Fraser
JOHN FENNEL	Clive Revill
EILEEN GRAHAM	Brenda Fricker
KARL	Michael Mellinger
HERR JUNGKE	George Herbert
ALLARDYCE	Patrick Monckton
LOTTERBY	Jonathan Coy
Photography	Ken Morgan
Producer	David Rose
Director	David Hare

Licking Hitler

1. EXT. HOUSE. DAY
An English country house. Perfect and undisturbed. Large and set among
woods. The sun behind it in the sky. Loudly a bird tweets.

2. EXT. DRIVE. DAY
A convoy of military vehicles comes noisily up the long drive.

3. INT. CORRIDOR. DAY
A corridor inside the house. At the end of the corridor we can see through to
the large hall where LANGLEY, *a uniformed army officer is standing. The*
sound of the convoy arriving. An elderly CHAUFFEUR *carries luggage out*
of the house. An even older MAID, *in black-and-white uniform, follows*
with more. LOTTERBY, *a young officer, comes into the house, salutes and*
begins reporting to LANGLEY. *All the time the camera is tracking back,*
drawn by the voice of ARCHIE MACLEAN.

ARCHIE: (VO) The question of Hess.
(*Pause.*)
Nobody really believes that Hess flew to Britain on the
Führer's instructions. Hess flew to Britain for one simple
reason; because he's a criminal lunatic.
(*The camera pans slowly round to a bare passage leading down to the*
servants' quarters. A few hunting and military pictures hang at
random on the cream walls. At the bottom of the passage the sun
shines brilliantly through the glass panes of the closed door of the gun
room, from which ARCHIE's *voice is coming.*)
Now what is frightening about Hess is not what he has
done. It is the fact he once found his way so easily into
Hitler's confidence. As loyal Germans we have to face the
fact that Adolf Hitler chooses to surround himself with
fools, arse-lickers, time-servers, traitors, megalomaniacs . . .
and men who wish to rape their own mothers.

4. INT. GUN ROOM. DAY

ARCHIE MACLEAN *is standing at one side of the room where the shotguns are kept. It is mostly very dirty, full of fishing rods, tennis rackets, golf clubs, mosquito nets, sola topees, nails, hammers, saws, croquet mallets, polo sticks, riding boots, skis, deerstalkers, wellingtons and husky jackets. There is a table piled with cartridges where* EILEEN GRAHAM *has cleared a space to take dictation. She is about 22, with very long legs and fashionably long and wavy hair. She is efficient, self-contained, lower-middle-class.* ARCHIE *is in his late twenties but already looks much more mature; squat, powerful, stocky, a Clydesider with a very precise manner.*

ARCHIE: God . . . God . . . when I think of the . . . (*Pause.* EILEEN *catches up on her dictation, then looks away and out of the window, while* ARCHIE *searches for the right word.*)
. . . worms. When I think of the worms, when I think of the cheapjacks, when I think of the human excrement that is even now clogging up the innermost councils of the Reich, when I think how badly divided our leaders are, how grossly they have miscalculated, how the pygmies scratch and . . .
(*Pause. Action again suspended.*)
. . . jostle . . . jostle round the Führer's teats, how the greybeard eunuchs and slug-like parvenues congest and clot the bloodstream of the nation, then I cry . . . Lord I cry for Germany.
(*He turns and looks at* EILEEN *still thinking. She looks up. Then he waves a hand.*)
Something like that.

5. EXT. COUNTRY LANE. DAY

Country lane in spring. A young girl of 19, struggling along the road, which is deserted, carrying two heavy suitcases which she has to put down every 50 yards. Her hair falls in front of her face. She is thin and very tired. ANNA.

6. INT. HALL. DAY

A large hall with a fine staircase. The front doors of the house have been flung open and opposite them the military vehicles are now parked and are being unloaded by SOLDIERS *under the direction of the* SERGEANT. *They are taking off office equipment, which they now bring into the house. Also waiting outside is an old Rolls-Royce. At the very centre of the hall* LORD MINTON *is sitting on his suitcase. He has a stick, a big black coat and is very old and ill. Around him, and taking no notice,* SOLDIERS *carry filing cabinets and wireless equipment through the hall and off down the corridor.*

LANGLEY *comes down the staircase. We see him to be in his thirties, thin, bony, with sleeked-down black hair and a very dry edge to his manner.* ALLARDYCE, *a young engineer, approaches him, carrying a green telephone.*

ALLARDYCE: The green line, sir—anywhere in particular?

LANGLEY: Best place is my study. I'll show you where that is.

> (ARCHIE *is standing in his shirt sleeves at the end of the corridor watching the arrivals.* LANGLEY *gestures to him.*)

Archie, can you . . .

> (LANGLEY *nods, then disappears with* ALLARDYCE *and the telephone equipment.* ARCHIE *looks across at the* CHAUFFEUR *who is coming back from the car.*)

ARCHIE: Is he ready?

> (*The* CHAUFFEUR *looks down at* LORD MINTON *and asks him a question in deaf and dumb language.* LORD MINTON *replies vociferously, then turns to* ARCHIE. *Gets up. He smiles and gestures wonderingly round the magnificent house. Then shrugs.* ARCHIE *hands him his cane and gloves.*)

7. EXT. STEPS OF THE HOUSE. DAY

ARCHIE *shakes* MINTON'S *hand and shouts at him.*

ARCHIE: Very kind. Of you. To lend us. Your place.

> (MINTON *turns and gets into the car, the door of which is held open for him by his* CHAUFFEUR.)

Tell him we appreciate his sacrifice. Having to spend the rest of the war in that squalid wee single end in Eaton Square.

(*The* CHAUFFEUR *smiles thinly as he closes the door, and goes round to drive away.* ANNA *arrives just in time to hear* ARCHIE *as he waves from the steps.*)

That's right Minton, you bugger off.

(ANNA *looks up at him.*)

ANNA: Is this Wendlesham?

ARCHIE: You were due yesterday.

ANNA: The train . . . it stopped for the night outside Aylesbury. Nobody knew why.

(*But* ARCHIE *has already turned to* LOTTERBY, *who is carrying a huge photograph of Goebbels into the house.* ARCHIE *seizes it.*)

And it's taken all day just to get . . .

LOTTERBY: Goebbels for you, sir.

(ARCHIE *smiles and goes into the house.*)

ARCHIE: We'll hang him in the study. Is that not what people do?

8. INT. HALL. DAY

ARCHIE *passes quickly through with* LOTTERBY *carrying the portrait of Goebbels.*

ARCHIE: Look at the face. Extraordinary face. The lips. (*They go off down the corridor.* ANNA *follows in through the door and looks round the hall which has suddenly emptied. She puts her bags down, looks round. Sudden quiet.*)

9. EXT. DRIVE. DAY

The military convoy disappears down the drive.

10. GUN ROOM. DAY

As before except now at the centre of the clutter is the large and magnificent portrait of Goebbels. ARCHIE *is standing at the window. It is darkening outside.* EILEEN *is sitting at the desk reading back typed dictation.*

EILEEN: The question of Hess, stop. Nobody believes that Hess came to Britain on the Führer's instructions, stop. Hess flew to Britain for one simple reason, colon. Because he's a criminal lunatic, stop.

(ANNA *is standing at the door. She has taken her coat off and has*

96

tidied up. She carries a huge volume under her arm. EILEEN
stops reading. ARCHIE *turns.*)

ARCHIE: I take it you've signed the Act. (ANNA *nods.*)
Sit down.
(ANNA *sits on a wooden chair among the tennis rackets.*)
Ihr Deutsch soll ausgezeichnet sein.

ANNA: Ja. Das war ja einfach für mich.

ARCHIE: Where did you learn?

ANNA: My family . . . my cousin was married to a German. I
spent my summers in Oberwesel. They had a *schloss* on the
Rhine.

ARCHIE: Who vetted you?

ANNA: Naval Intelligence. My uncle is Second Sea Lord at the
Admiralty.

ARCHIE: I see.

ANNA: I also have a cousin who's high-up in . . .

ARCHIE: Och yes, I can imagine.
(*There is a pause.* ARCHIE *looks at* ANNA.)
Well, there's nothing for you yet. But we do need somebody
to make the tea.

11. INT. KITCHEN. EVENING

*A large bare room with a gas range. The only provisions in view are a
packet of tea, a packet of sugar and a bottle of milk.* ANNA *comes in, looks
around, then takes a saucepan over to the tap. We can hear* EILEEN *in the
distance repeating the Hess speech.* ANNA *pauses uncertainly at the tap,
then turns back, takes a decision. She confidently empties the whole packet
of tea into the saucepan and pours on to it a good hard gush of cold water.
She then puts the pan on to the gas and lights it.*

12. INT. CORRIDOR. EVENING

Empty. Gun room door open.

ARCHIE: (VO) I'll do the blackout, it's a'right.
(EILEEN *appears from the gun room, looks puzzled down the
corridor, then goes one door down to the kitchen. Goes in.*)

13. INT. KITCHEN. EVENING

The tea is now boiling, ANNA *is staring at it. She looks up at* EILEEN *as soon as she comes in.* EILEEN *at once takes it off the stove, amazed, and looks at the empty packet.*

EILEEN: That's a week's ration.

ANNA: I've never had to.

(*She is beginning to cry.*)

EILEEN: No.

ANNA: Just can't.

14. INT. BEDROOM. NIGHT

A darkened room, plain, once a servant's bedroom. An iron bed. ANNA *lying awake in the dark. Then quietly she slips the covers off and runs across to her suitcase at the far side of the room. Takes out her battered, yellowing teddy bear. Returns to bed with him. Stops in front of the bed.*

ANNA: Which side do you want?

15. INT. DRAWING ROOM. DAY

A magnificent yellow room. High windows. Bright daylight. Armchairs and sofas. Superb full-length portraits on the walls. At one end LANGLEY *has set up a table behind which he and* FENNEL *sit.* FENNEL *is almost 40, fat, boyish, an enthusiast, an intellectual enjoying his war. Scattered round the room are a mixture of* PLAINCLOTHES PEOPLE, ENGINEERS *and* OFFICERS *from the three Services. Next to* ANNA *on a sofa is* KARL, *heavy, dark-jowelled, bewildered. He seems to understand nothing of what is going on.*

FENNEL: This is a research unit within the Political Warfare Executive. How the rest of that department functions is none of your concern. I am your only contact with the world outside and I don't expect to visit you very often. I'm afraid you will know very little about the success or failure of your work. You are throwing stones into a pond which is a very long way away. And there will be almost no ripples. So your job must be to keep your heads down and just . . . keep at it, even though you'll have almost no idea of the effect you're having.

(KARL *leans across the sofa and whispers to* ANNA.)

KARL: Ich verstehe nicht.

ANNA: (*Whispers in German*) Moment.

FENNEL: Perhaps even when the war is over you will not know what good you did.

(FENNEL *smiles.*)

16. INT. DRAWING ROOM. DAY

ANNA *leans alone against a window frame. Everyone is now standing in cocktail positions. Two* MAIDS *pass between groups of people pouring out beer from big, stoppered 2-pint bottles. In one group stand* FENNEL, LANGLEY, ALLARDYCE.

FENNEL: I suppose you'd been hoping to represent your country.

LANGLEY: That's right. I was aiming for the 1940 Olympics.

(*He smiles.*)

FENNEL: But you still have your blue?

LANGLEY: Half-blue.

FENNEL: Fencing is a half-blue?

LANGLEY: That's right. But I'm still hoping for national honour. I mean, after the war.

(*They smile.* ARCHIE *is sitting alone on the sofa staring across the room at* ANNA. ANNA *raises the pint mug to her lips but takes as little as possible. She is very self-conscious and lonely. The* FENNEL *conversation has moved on.*)

FENNEL: The boys on *The Times* actually got hold of an onion.

LANGLEY: Good Lord.

FENNEL: Can you imagine? Someone actually gave them one. A whole onion. Great big thing. So they auctioned it among the staff. Went to the night editor for £4 3s. 4d.

ALLARDYCE: Well.

LANGLEY: Worth it.

(*Now* FENNEL *seems to catch* ANNA's *eye. She looks away.*)

FENNEL: Certainly. Of course.

(*A gong sounds. The room goes silent, caught for a moment as they stand.*)

17. INT. DINING ROOM. DAY

The Unit sits round a large dinner table, overhung with chandeliers. The OLDER MAID *dollops mashed potato on to each plate as the*

YOUNG MAID *passes with an ashet on which sits a piece of pork luncheon meat in the shape of a tin. She puts it down at the head of the table, and as the top seat is unoccupied,* ARCHIE *rises and gravely begins to carve the luncheon meat. It makes a succulent, unpleasant noise.* ANNA *looks out of the window to the drive where* LANGLEY *is talking animatedly to* FENNEL *and a* NAVAL COMMANDER. *You can just hear them speaking.*

FENNEL: Goodbye. Good luck. I'll try and get down in a couple of months.

> (FENNEL *and the* COMMANDER *climb into the car, gathering up piles of paper from off the back seat. They look to* ANNA *romantic and attractive.* FENNEL'S DRIVER *drives them away.*
>
> *An uneasy silence as the Unit eat.* KARL *leans to* ANNA *and whispers in German. Apologetically,* ANNA *speaks.*)

ANNA: He would like to know . . . what exactly we're all doing here.

> (ARCHIE *looks up from his food.*)

ARCHIE: Tell him it's a wireless station. Like the BBC.

18. INT. GUN ROOM. DAY

ARCHIE *at the window.* EILEEN *with her dictation pad.* ANNA *and* KARL *sitting useless at the other side of the room.*

EILEEN: The question of Hess.

ARCHIE: The question of Hess.

> (*He taps his knuckles on the windowpane in a gesture of frustration.*)

ANNA: Perhaps if you told us more about it we would be able to help.

> (EILEEN *smiles.* ANNA *watches as* ARCHIE *turns and stares at her.*)

ARCHIE: The game is. We are a radio station . . .

ANNA: Yes.

ARCHIE: Broadcasting to Germany. My job is to script the broadcasts. Your job is to interpret them.

ANNA: I see.

KARL: Was sagt er?

ANNA: (*In German*) Propaganda.

ARCHIE: Yes.

> (*Pause.*)

ARCHIE: We are to pretend to be two German army officers

100

stationed a thousand miles apart sending coded
messages to each other nightly over short-wave radio.
When the messages have been sent, the idea is that one of
our officers—'Otto'—will relax, he will talk more frankly,
he will add his own personal comments on the conduct of
the war. And those comments will not be complimentary to
the Nazi leaders.

ANNA: I see.

ARCHIE: Does that make sense to you?

ANNA: Of course. But it does seem a little elaborate.

(*A moment.* ARCHIE *looks beadily at* ANNA.)

ARCHIE: You fight a war, you expect propaganda, you expect
  your enemy to tell you lies. Right?

(*He moves across the room towards them.*)

So people spend a good deal of their time on their guard.
Now the beauty of this idea is that when we make our first
broadcast tonight, maybe ten or fifteen people, radio hams
mostly, will twiddle their dials and stumble on it. But
because they have found us by accident, and because they
appear to be eavesdropping on a purely private
conversation, and that conversation is indubitably between
loyal army officers on their own side . . . they will be
inclined to trust everything we say. And from that trust our
influence will grow.

(ANNA *looks at* ARCHIE, *then nods at* KARL.)

ANNA: Is he one of the officers?

(ARCHIE *nods.*)

Who is he really?

ARCHIE: He's a Jew. From Frankfurt.

ANNA: Shall I tell him?

(ARCHIE *nods.* ANNA *turns to* KARL. *As* ARCHIE *speaks* ANNA
  translates.)

ARCHIE: He will be playing the part of Otto, a loyal Prussian
  officer, broadcasting to an old friend in another part of
  Germany . . .

ANNA: (*Translating consecutively*) Sie sollen die Rolle von Otto
  spielen, einem treuen preussischen Offizier, der mit einem

101

altern Kameraden in einem anderen Teil Deutschlands
ein Rundfunkgespräch führt.

KARL: Sie meinen, ich soll Theater spielen?

ANNA: Ja.

ARCHIE: The character of the Prussian must be authentic . . .

ANNA: Er muss authentisch sein.

(ARCHIE *is staring at* ANNA, *who has lost her nervousness for the
first time.*)

ARCHIE: His language will therefore be rough . . .

ANNA: Er spricht sehr roh.

ARCHIE: Corrosive . . .

ANNA: Abrupt.

ARCHIE: Obscene.

(ANNA *does not look up. A pause.*)

ANNA: Obszön.

(KARL *looks up.*)

19. INT. BILLIARD ROOM. NIGHT

*The room has been converted into a wireless station, but signs of its
original function remain. Racks of cues stand on the walls, and there is a
prominent scoreboard. A green leather top has been laid over the baize.*

*Microphones have been placed at either end of the table, beside green
light bulbs which flash to cue the broadcaster. At one end is* KARL, *at the
other* HERR JUNGKE. *He is a small, rather effete old man with pursed
lips. In the middle, like a tennis umpire, sits* ALLARDYCE *controlling the
equipment.*

Along the side of the room sit the rest of the Unit watching: ARCHIE,
ANNA, EILEEN, LANGLEY.

ALLARDYCE: Stand by, please.

(*A red light comes on and* ALLARDYCE *nods at* KARL *who is looking
more than usually nervous and distraught.*)

ALLARDYCE: You have the air.

(LANGLEY *makes a sign at* KARL *to sit forward. The green light
comes on silently in front of him.*)

KARL: Hier Otto-Abend Eins . . . Hier Otto-Abend Eins.

(KARL's *light goes out. He sits back. At the other end of the table*
JUNGKE's *light comes on. He now cups one hand over his ear*

instinctively in response to KARL.)

JUNGKE: Ja . . . Otto . . . ich empfange . . . hast du 'ne Meldung?
(*A moment, then his light goes out. He sits back with an expression of relief. At the other end* KARL *becomes more apprehensive then ever. His light is on.* ALLARDYCE *beckons at him.*)

KARL: Jawohl. Die Meldung lautet. Mitzi muss ihren Vater treffen. Mitzi muss ihren Vater treffen.
(KARL's *light goes out.* JUNGKE's *light comes on. We see down the whole length of the billiard table, two ludicrous figures pretending to be miles apart.*)

JUNGKE: Verstanden. Na, Otto, was hältst du denn von der Flucht von Hess?
(*The light bulbs change.* KARL *flinches.*)

KARL: Ach ja, die Sache mit Hess. Tja, also . . .
(*He seems to have lost his place.* ARCHIE *puts his head in his hands.* ANNA *looks away.*)
Niemand glaubt, Hess sei auf Befehl des Führers nach England geflogen. Nein nein, er ist aus einem ganz anderen Grund nach England geflogen.
(ARCHIE *gets up from his seat.*)
Der Grund ist—er ist ein grosser Verbrecher, ein Wahnsinniger.

20. INT. TRANSMISSION ROOM. NIGHT

A disc-cutting machine is the next room. Over it sits an ENGINEER *wiping the floss from the disc as it cuts. Behind him stands* LOTTERBY.

KARL: (VO) Der Erschrekende an Hess ist nicht was er gemacht hat, sondern die Tatsache dass er so leicht ein Vertrauter Hitlers werden konnte. Als treue Deutsche müssen wir uns damit abfinden, dass Adolf Hitler bereit ist, Idioten um sich zu dulden . . .

21. EXT. HOUSE. NIGHT

The house from outside sitting confidently in the English countryside. The moon beyond. Distorted across the airwaves comes the continuous sound of KARL, *now ranting falteringly but with increasing vehemence. Some rabbits pass across the lawn.*

KARL: (VO) . . . Archlecker, Verbrecher, Verräter, solche die an
Grössenwahn leiden, oder die ihre eigenen Mütter
vergewaltigen wollen.

22. INT. BILLIARD ROOM. NIGHT

JUNGKE *waves at* KARL. KARL *waves back.*

JUNGKE: Auf wiedersehen.

> (*His light goes out.* ALLARDYCE *turns to* KARL.)

KARL: Auf wiedersehen.

> (*His light goes out. He sits back.* ARCHIE *walks straight out of the
> room. Silence.* KARL *spreads his palms on the table.*)

Am sorry.

> (LANGLEY *acknowledges this with a nod.* KARL *speaks with terrible
> seriousness and difficulty.*)

Will be good.

LANGLEY: Yes.

KARL: All Jews . . . good at showbiz.

LANGLEY: Yes. (*He gets up and smiles.*) All right everyone.

23. INT. HALL. NIGHT

The Unit comes quietly into the hall and disperses upstairs, ANNA *and*
EILEEN *walking up together.* LANGLEY *crosses with* JUNGKE *to the front
door where* LOTTERBY *is waiting with* JUNGKE'S *coat.*

LOTTERBY: Take Herr Jungke back, sir.

LANGLEY: Thank you.

> (JUNGKE *confides in* LANGLEY *as he puts his coat on.*)

JUNGKE: The boy is nervous.

LANGLEY: Yes.

JUNGKE: But also the script is not good. The writing . . . (*Rubs his
fingers together*) . . . not savage enough.

> (*A pause.* LANGLEY *remains expressionless.*)

LANGLEY: We'll try again tomorrow. Thank you for coming.
Goodnight.

> (*He reaches for the unseen light switch by the door and we are
> plunged into darkness.*)

24. EXT. SKY. NIGHT
Clouds move quickly across the moon.

25. INT. BEDROOM. NIGHT
As before, but this time ANNA *is asleep. Then suddenly the door crashes open, and* ARCHIE *bursts into the room carrying a bottle of scotch.*
ARCHIE: I'll smash a bloody bottle in yer if yer bloody come near me.
(*He slips and falls at once to the floor. The bottle smashes. Silence.*)

26. INT. CORRIDOR. NIGHT
In the moonlight ANNA's *door opens and she appears dragging* ARCHIE's *body out into the upstairs corridor. Then, when she's got him out, she turns him to point the way the corridor goes. He does not wake. Then she goes back in. A moment later she comes out with a blanket which she lays over him. She goes back into her room, closes the door.*

27. INT. BEDROOM. DAY
Morning light at the window. ANNA *gets out of bed. Avoids the broken glass on the floor. Takes away the chair she has jammed under the doorhandle. She involuntarily puts one arm over her chest as she opens the door. The corridor is deserted. Even the blanket has gone.*

28. INT. DINING ROOM. DAY
ARCHIE *sits alone at the far end of the table with a bottle of milk and a plain glass.* ANNA *goes over to the sideboard. On the hotplate there is a kettle, a pan and a tin. She opens it. Powdered eggs. She attempts normality.*
ANNA: Can I make you some egg?
ARCHIE: I've had yer tea. I'd want inoculation before I tried yer egg.
ANNA: Look, I'm quite prepared not to mention the fact . . .
ARCHIE: (*Shouts*) What?
(ANNA *looks at him and walks out of the room.*)

29. INT. HALL. DAY
ANNA *comes out into the deserted hall. At the bottom of the staircase a*

teleprinter machine is clattering out information. Then a voice comes from a distant wireless.

VOICE: This is the first news bulletin of the day and Joseph McLeod reading it. The retreat of the defeated Italian army goes on. General Wavell's message to his troops . . .

(ANNA *stands alone in the middle of the hall.*)

ANNA: Somebody talk to me.

30. MONTAGE SEQUENCE ONE

At once we hear Chopin's Waltz No. 3 in A Minor. A piano segment, no more than thirty seconds. Under it we see the following images: ARCHIE *standing watching the rain coming down outside the window;* ALLARDYCE *looking regretfully away as* KARL *blunders through another broadcast;* ANNA *and* EILEEN *laughing together as* EILEEN *elaborately shows* ANNA *how to make a cup of tea;* LANGLEY *and* ALLARDYCE *playing croquet on the lawn as* EILEEN *and* ANNA *sit watching.* LOTTERBY *stands behind them and commentates. Long cool drinks are being sipped;* ANNA *before she goes to bed putting the chair against her door. Fade. The Chopin ends.*

31. INT. PASSAGE. DAY

Outside the gun room. Most of the sporting gear has been moved into the passage from which no one has had time to move it. It is oddly piled alongside overspill from inside the office. There is a pair of skis by the door. Nailed on to the door is a trophy, a Nazi notice board: JUDEN BETRETEN DIESEN ORT AUF EIGENE GEFAHR. The sound of EILEEN's *typewriter as* ANNA *walks quickly down the passage and into the gun room.*

32. INT. GUN ROOM. DAY

EILEEN *at work on a huge pile of notes.* ANNA *comes in.*

ANNA: Langley wants us. There's a morning conference.

EILEEN: I've still got all this stuff to do.

ANNA: They're going into Russia.

EILEEN: Who?

ANNA: The Germans.

EILEEN: Into Russia. What for?

106

ANNA: To make us work even harder, I suppose.

>   (EILEEN *smiles*.)

33. INT. LANGLEY'S OFFICE. DAY

A room in the front of the house. Once a gentleman's study and library, now serving as LANGLEY'S *office, it has a large open fireplace and cleared desks. It is clean, manly and well ordered. Flowers in vases.* LANGLEY *sits behind his desk opposite* ARCHIE. *At one side* EILEEN *sits taking dictation; on the other side sits* ANNA. LANGLEY *is at his most severe.*

LANGLEY: This discussion to be noted, minuted, dated 10th June 1941.

>   (EILEEN's *shorthand follows*.)
>
>   We have it from the War Cabinet that Hitler is invading Russia within the next two weeks. I needn't stress how important this news is to our work. It's a military step of extraordinary foolishness, Hitler himself counsels against it in *Mein Kampf*, and it gives us exactly the opportunity we've been looking for to cast doubt on Germany's war leadership. Our loyal German officer therefore is now in a position to condemn the step as national suicide. He can then go on to question the whole direction of the war.
>
>   (*Pause*.)

ARCHIE: May I ask a question, Will?

LANGLEY: Of course.

ARCHIE: Surely if there's a possibility of national suicide, that's something we'd be wanting to encourage, no? (*He smiles*.)

LANGLEY: I'm sorry, I don't see your point.

ARCHIE: You see, I can't help looking at it another way. Your idea is nice, Will, I mean it's simple anyway, but surely one of the things we've learnt . . . attack the leadership direct and it always sounds like propaganda. And anything that sounds like propaganda is not good propaganda.

LANGLEY: Go on.

ARCHIE: I'd say if they're going to do something foolish, we should encourage them. I mean, let's have Otto right behind the idea.

LANGLEY: But you can't justify it, Archie. Otto's a military man . . .

ARCHIE: Look, Otto says . . .

LANGLEY: He'd know that going into Russia is insane. I mean, a war on two fronts.

ARCHIE: Look, Otto says . . . Otto says the real enemy of Germany has always been Bolshevism. And now the army is getting a chance to begin its real fight. But. It is hard to fight Bolshevism abroad, when there are known Bolsheviks inside the Nazi Party. So. The loyal German is happy to die in Russia, but he is not happy if there is any evidence of subversion at home. And anybody . . . anybody at all who for whatever reason dares to oppose the Russian venture, or fails to support it with every sinew of their body is by definition . . . a Bolshevik. (*He smiles.*) Do y'see, everybody? Red-baiting! (*He laughs and claps his hands together.*) Anyone who speaks out is branded as a Bolshevik. Criticism silenced. Millions die.

(*Pause.* LANGLEY *stares at him.*)

Well? Is that no' what ye want?

34. INT. GUN ROOM. NIGHT

Blacked-out windows. A single green light. EILEEN *has a single sheet of paper in her hand, which she reads out.* ARCHIE *is sitting on the desk.* LANGLEY, ANNA *are watching.* KARL *is tucked away, his lips moving slightly as* EILEEN *reads. There is a new concentration in the work.* EILEEN *reads well.*

EILEEN: Many will die. Many will be happy to die on the road to Moscow as long as they feel they have the efforts of the whole nation concentrated behind them. For those who stay at home have a duty too. They have a duty to keep morale high, to silence dissent.

(ARCHIE *nods at* LANGLEY *to signal approval of the idea.*)

There will not be enough food this winter, there will not be enough clothes. Everyone must therefore try to discover those Party members who are taking more than their rations. Everyone will have to be vigilant, everyone will have to be a spy. It is a great adventure. We must all be

ruthless in its pursuit. Goodnight my friend. My dear,
dear friend.

(*She looks up. They look at her, awed.*)

35. INT. BILLIARD ROOM. NIGHT

The red light goes on. KARL *bends forward. He is transformed. We follow
his delivery—ironic, witty, inflected. Sweat pours from him. His voice is
much deeper than before.*

KARL: Viele werden sterben. Viele werden froh sein auf dem
Wege nach Moskau zu sterben, solange sie wissen, dass das
ganze Volk ihnen beisteht.

(*We look at the Unit sitting at the side, as if deeply moved by what
he is saying.*)

Aber die, die zu Hause bleiben, haben auch eine Aufgabe.
Ihre Aufgabe ist es, die Moral des Volkes zu heben und
Gegner zum Schweigen zu bringen. Es wird in diesem
Winter nicht genug zu essen geben, nicht genug Kleidung.

(ARCHIE *smiles. We go back to* KARL.)

Jeder muss also versuchen herauszufinden, welche
Parteimiglieder mehr als ihre Rationen bekommen. Jeder
muss wachsam sein. Jeder muss Spion sein. Es ist ein
grosses Abenteuer. Wir müssen rücksichtslos sein. Gute
Nacht lieber Freund, mein lieber, lieber Freund.

(*The red light goes off and* KARL *takes off his glasses.* LANGLEY
smiles.)

LANGLEY: Superb!

36. INT. HALL. NIGHT

At once Chopin again. Odd, lilting, deft. LANGLEY *and* ARCHIE *seen
from behind going down corridor together.*

ARCHIE: We've hit a vein.

LANGLEY: We have. More again tomorrow?

ARCHIE: Certainly.

LANGLEY: This Russian business . . . could be the making
of us.

(*As they turn into the drawing room,* ARCHIE *uncharacteristically
performs a tiny dance step.*)

37. INT. DRAWING ROOM. NIGHT

JUNGKE *sits playing Chopin. His face is angelic, his feet barely touch the pedals. The Steinway has been pulled out from the wall, and the Unit has flopped down round the room.* EILEEN *is reading* Wellington Wendy, LANGLEY *is reading* The Times. *The* ENGINEERS *are playing chess.* ANNA *sits staring on a sofa as behind her* ARCHIE *moves very slowly, decanter in hand. He stops immediately behind her, pours out a glass very steadily and moves on. She does not turn.* JUNGKE *leans in to perform an intricate arpeggio. Then* LOTTERBY *appears at the door with* JUNGKE'S *coat.*

LOTTERBY: The car for Herr Jungke, sir.

>   (JUNGKE *stops playing.* LANGLEY *gets up from his seat, speaks slowly to him.*)

LANGLEY: We have something for you.

>   (LOTTERBY *crosses to the piano and helps* JUNGKE *up as* LANGLEY *goes to the sideboard where a bottle sits on a tray with a little dish beside it.* LOTTERBY *brings* JUNGKE *back and sits him in* LANGLEY'S *empty chair.* LANGLEY *ceremoniously carries the tray and sets it down beside* JUNGKE.)

LANGLEY: Sambuca.

JUNGKE: Do you have . . . a coffee bean?

>   (LANGLEY *takes the dish and puts one coffee bean in the liquid, then takes out a box of matches and sets light to it.* JUNGKE *looks at the flame.*)

JUNGKE: It is payment enough. Thank you.

>   (LANGLEY *looks up at* LOTTERBY.)

LANGLEY: Ian, would you take Herr Jungke back to the internment camp?

LOTTERBY: Sir.

38. INT. HALL. NIGHT

JUNGKE *is being escorted out by* LANGLEY. LOTTERBY *waits for them.*

JUNGKE: It's not too bad. I have to be in solitary because of this work but there are compensations. I have books, you know. And I had a letter once.

>   (ANNA *and* EILEEN *cross the hall and go upstairs on their way to bed.*)

EILEEN: Archie's drunk again.

ANNA: Why does he drink so much?

EILEEN: I don't know. Fleet Street, I suppose. They all do.

ANNA: Was he a journalist?

39. INT. STAIRS. NIGHT

ANNA *and* EILEEN *on the servants' stairs.*

EILEEN: By the time the war came he was on one of the big
national dailies. Fought his way up.

ANNA: From?

EILEEN: Poverty. Terrible. He comes from Glasgow, from the
Red Clyde. You must know that.

ANNA: I don't know anything.

40. INT. BEDROOM. NIGHT

ANNA *comes into her bedroom. Closes the door. She then picks up the chair
to put it under the handle. But then pauses with the chair in her hand.
Turns. Puts the chair back where it came from. Goes instead into the
bathroom.*

41. INT. BEDROOM. NIGHT

As before. ANNA*'s face, asleep. We are very close.*

ARCHIE: (VO) Woman.

(*A moment, then* ANNA *opens her eyes. She does not move. The sound
of ripping material.*)

(VO) I'm at yer feet.

(ANNA *scrambles up the bed and stands on top of it. By this time she
can make out the figure of* ARCHIE *at the bottom of the bed. He is
very serious and very drunk.*)

The Scotsman's approach to the art a' love-makin'.

(*Pause.*) The Scot makes love wi' a broken bottle. An' a
great deal a' screamin'. (*Pause.*) There'll be a moment while
I take off ma clothes.

(*He disappears beneath the end of the bed. There is a pause.* ANNA
peers forward, into the dark.)

111

42. INT. BEDROOM. NIGHT

ANNA *lying in bed with the sheet pulled up around her. She is soaked in
sweat, her hair in strands. There is a light on in the bathroom and the door
is ajar. You can see a trousered leg and hear the sound of water in a bowl.*
ANNA *barely turns towards the figure.*

ANNA: I literally didn't know there was such a thing as an
electricity bill. I was sheltered, I suppose. Where we live we
just always left the lights on. I assumed the electricity just
came . . . it just came and you paid your taxes and you got
your light. Then the other day I was talking to Eileen and
she said electricity prices had risen, and I said, you mean,
you have to pay? For what you use? You have to pay? Gas,
electricity, water. It had never occurred to me. (*Silence. She
shivers.*) Archie. I am trying to learn.

(*The light goes out in the bathroom.* ARCHIE *walks silently through
the bedroom, opens the door and goes out.* ANNA *alone.*)

43. INT. KITCHEN. DAY

Daylight flooding in at the kitchen window. ANNA *is sitting on the table
with her back to us as* EILEEN *carefully steams open envelopes over a
boiling kettle. She then sorts the letters out into two piles.*

EILEEN: (*Sorting through letters*) German . . . German for you . . .
English for me . . . German . . . English.

(ANNA *casually picks one up.*)

ANNA: Who wrote them?

EILEEN: Just ordinary people in Germany writing to their
relatives in the States.

ANNA: I didn't know they were allowed to.

EILEEN: Why not? America's neutral.

ANNA: Then how did we get hold of them?

EILEEN: Not that neutral, apparently. English . . .

ANNA: What are we meant to do with them?

EILEEN: You'll have to ask Genius.

ANNA: Is he down?

EILEEN: In the office.

ANNA: Ah.

(ANNA *goes.* EILEEN *continues to read her letters.*)

EILEEN: Whoops. Somebody's dead.

44. INT. GUN ROOM. DAY

ARCHIE *at his desk writing flowingly with a fountain pen. Bright morning light behind him. Around him fresh supplies of office stationery, including two piles of files almost ceiling-high. On one wall is pinned a new map of Germany. He does not look up as ANNA comes in. She stands at the door with a fistful of letters.*

ANNA: I want to know what to do with these.

    (ARCHIE *looks at her, referring to the piles of stationery.*)

ARCHIE: I shall be opening files on named individuals. While their army is in Russia we shall be looking for examples of favouritism at home. How Nazi Party officials get more food, get more clothes, than ordinary people. How they get sugar. How they get fruit. How they get wine. How they give parties in private rooms where cakes full of raisins and marzipan are eaten. Outrageous things. You have to comb through these letters, and open files on any named official, you have to pick out from the gossip any hard fact, any details of their way of life, any indiscretion, any sign that they're enjoying themselves more than their brothers-in-arms. This way we drive a wedge between the Party and the people. We broadcast real names, plausible offences, backed up with thorough research.

    (*He looks at* ANNA, *then returns to writing.*)

ANNA: And when we've finished with the letters . . . ?

ARCHIE: Yes.

ANNA: Do we send them on?

    (ARCHIE *stares at her.*)

ARCHIE: Yes. We send them on.

    (ARCHIE *returns to writing.* ANNA *moves across the room sharply and puts the letters down on his desk.*)

ANNA: Mr Maclean.

ARCHIE: Yes.

    (*This time he does not look up at* ANNA.)

ANNA: I have to go to the medicine cupboard.

ARCHIE: Yes.

ANNA: I have some bruises.

ARCHIE: Yes.

> (*Nothing.* ANNA *turns to go.*)

45. INT. LANGLEY'S OFFICE. DAY

FENNEL *in a big chair with a pot of coffee. He looks more crumpled and effusive than ever. He talks in a fast stream which* LANGLEY *can barely intercept.*

FENNEL: We now have four stations like yours, Will, each pretending to be an individual broadcasting from within Germany. Of course, none of this would be necessary if we could persuade the BBC to take a less literal attitude to what they like to call the truth, but I'm afraid that they do go on insisting that when the Navy says it's sunk a sub, it does actually have to have sunk a sub. So I can't see us getting much joy out of them. So what I'd like to do is co-ordinate all intelligence outlets, and start a Rumour Committee which will take charge of all misleading information, so we don't find ourselves with lots of little rumours popping up all over the place, but put all our efforts into good big sharp vicious rumours that really do the job. . . .

> (*A knock at the door.*)

LANGLEY: Come in.

> (ANNA *enters.*)

ANNA: I'm sorry, I just want the medicine chest.

LANGLEY: Yes, of course. Come in.

> (LANGLEY *goes to get it down from a high cabinet.* FENNEL *goes on, ignoring* ANNA.)

FENNEL: It'll be a high-level committee; Sandy, Gargs, Freddy, if we have to, God help us, weekly meetings, decide who to go for . . .

LANGLEY: Yes.

FENNEL: Mostly the smaller fish, but go hard . . .

LANGLEY: Yes.

FENNEL: It's the little chap, the local leader we can really destroy, smears, innuendo, well co-ordinated . . .

LANGLEY: Yes.

FENNEL: Anyway we'll send you Rumour Directives. They'll
come on G2s, of course. When you get the G2, for Christ's
sake don't forget to cross-file.

(LANGLEY *hands a white box with a red cross to* ANNA.)

LANGLEY: Here you are.

ANNA: Thank you.

FENNEL: I hope you're settling down all right, my dear. Don't
find it all too high-powered.

(ANNA *smiles, not knowing what to say. She clutches the box.*)
Your uncle was very angry with me. Said I'd sent you to
work for a savage.

(ANNA *looks at* LANGLEY.)

LANGLEY: I think he means Maclean.

ANNA: I see.

FENNEL: That's right.

(ANNA *opens the medicine box and searches through it. They look at
her as if expecting her to say more.*) The Celtic race, you know:
a cloven-hoofed people. They do seem to be fighting quite a
different war.

ANNA: He seems . . . he just seems a very extraordinary man to
me.

(*She turns and looks at them defiantly. Then refers to a bottle.*)
Is this Dettol?

LANGLEY: That's what it says.

46. INT. BEDROOM. DAY

ANNA *sitting on the edge of her bed. She lifts her skirt up and undoes a
suspender. Pulls down her stocking. On her upper thigh, scratch and bruise
marks. She applies the Dettol with cotton wool. Tears come into her eyes.
She works down her thigh. Tears flow now, silently. Without sobbing, she
just lets the tears run down her cheek.*

47. MONTAGE SEQUENCE TWO

Chopin again. The same segment. Under it we see: EILEEN *hard at work
at night, typing furiously;* KARL *broadcasting, a look of extreme
vindictiveness colouring his face; The Unit sitting round a dinner table
heavy with Christmas decoration.* ANNA *comes into the dining-room with a*

soufflé she has obviously just cooked. Everyone applauds. ANNA *getting out of bed in the morning. She removes an empty whisky bottle from the bedside table and takes it to the wardrobe. There she sets it in a rank next to six other empty bottles which are stacked on a high shelf next to her teddy. Fade. Chopin ends.*

48. INT. PASSAGE. DAY

Now almost impassable. A line of filing cabinets is banked along one wall. Opposite, several thousand loose files and complete editions of German and English newspapers. LANGLEY *comes down with a file and finds* ANNA *sitting on the floor in the corridor doing her work. She is wrapped in many sweaters against the cold. He refers into the gun room.*

LANGLEY: What's happening?

ANNA: One of his moods. What's that?

LANGLEY: German prisoners of war. Interrogated by Intelligence. Very gratifying. Look.

(*He opens the file and hands it to* ANNA. *From inside the room you can hear* EILEEN's *typewriter and* ARCHIE's *odd bad-tempered grunt.*)

They report a run on clothing in Berlin. It's impossible to buy an overcoat because of rumours that Nazi Party officials are soon to get special clothing privileges.

ANNA: Amazing.

LANGLEY: They're issuing denials but to no effect. All our own work. It's proof someone's listening. I'll show it to him.

ANNA: He wouldn't want to know. It would spoil the game.

(*They smile.*)

ARCHIE: (*VO, rudely*) Anna.

49. INT. GUN ROOM. DAY

The room is now a fat stew of paperwork. Towers of documents take up most of the room. ARCHIE *is strained and tired.* EILEEN, *who like* ANNA *is well wrapped, is barely keeping her patience with him.* ANNA *comes in.*

ARCHIE: I have chosen Cologne. I have chosen the Burgomaster in Cologne. Now what do we have?

(ANNA *looks round the room confused.*)

ANNA: Eileen, is Cologne in the lavatory?

EILEEN: No, no it's over there somewhere.

(ANNA *heads where* EILEEN *pointed, flicks through.*)

ARCHIE: Eileen. Prisoner interrogation. Anything we have from the cages to do with Cologne.

(EILEEN *gets up and goes out.*)

50. INT. PASSAGE. DAY

LANGLEY *is standing listening outside the door, unseen by* ARCHIE. *As* EILEEN *comes out to get a file, she turns back towards the room and mimes machine-gunning* ARCHIE *to death.* LANGLEY *smiles and squeezes her arm.* EILEEN *just nods and sets to work.* LANGLEY *heads off down the corridor, casually tossing the file he has brought on to a random pile.*

51. INT. GUN ROOM. DAY

ANNA *lays out what she's collected on* ARCHIE's *desk, taking it all from one fat file.*

ANNA: Street directory. Train timetable. Party structure.

ARCHIE: Ah.

(*He takes that out and studies it.*)

ANNA: Bus timetables. Guide to the museum. Plan of the sewers, any use?

(*She smiles; he takes no notice.*)

ARCHIE: His name is Duffendorf. Lutz Duffendorf, Burgomaster of Cologne, please.

(*This last to* ANNA, *who goes to a wall cabinet for a file-card system.* EILEEN *meanwhile is back from the corridor.*)

EILEEN: Cologne's pretty good. Eighteen separate interrogations. Three or four look good.

ANNA: (*To herself*) D—Duffendorf.

ARCHIE: I need a woman, Eileen. Find me a woman of doubtful reputation.

EILEEN: I'll see.

(*As she goes to search,* ANNA *returns, with a white card.*)

ANNA: Lutz Duffendorf. Age 43. Bookseller's son. Married. No children.

ARCHIE: No children.

ANNA: His wife is blind.

ARCHIE: Wife blind. How wonderful.

ANNA: There's a picture.

(*She detaches a newspaper photo from the card and shows it to*
ARCHIE, *holding a pencil over the man's face. An official dinner at
which a group of Germans are conspicuously well fed. Duffendorf is
fat and slack.* ARCHIE *stares at him. Meanwhile,* EILEEN *has found
a suitable detail.*)

EILEEN: Someone in the parachute regiment mentions a
greengrocer, and his wife, in Blumenstrasse. She sounds
what you're looking for.

ARCHIE: Good.

(*He reaches down behind his desk and gets out three large volumes.*)
Krafft-Ebing. Havelock Ellis. And Kleinwort's *Dictionary of
Sexual Perversion*. Start at the index, right?

(*He hands the dictionary to* ANNA. EILEEN *is about to protest.*)

EILEEN: Is this . . . ?

(*But* ARCHIE *just looks at her and she turns away.* ANNA *opens the
book, then begins reading dispassionately.*)

ANNA: Fantasies?

ARCHIE: Yes.

ANNA: Male fantasies. Judge. Air pilot. Hanged man. Horse.
Snake charmer. Roman Catholic Priest . . .

ARCHIE: All right. Off fantasies.

ANNA: Fetishes?

ARCHIE: Yes.

ANNA: Food. Rope. Rubber. Leather . . .

ARCHIE: Look up leather.

(ANNA *looks at* ARCHIE, *but he cuts her off before she speaks.*)
It will do. Eileen.

(EILEEN *waits, pad in hand, patiently.* ANNA *looks up the reference.*)
You won't believe this, old friend, what . . .

EILEEN: Duffendorf.

ARCHIE: . . . what Duffendorf's been up to. Everyone in Cologne
is talking about what the telegram boy saw when he looked
through the letterbox trying to deliver. What he saw was
the Burgomaster trying to deliver to Frau . . .

ANNA: (*Not looking up*) That pun won't translate.

EILEEN: Ilse Schmidt.

ARCHIE: Trying to deliver to Frau Ilse Schmidt. Well we know how many people have been down that particular path before. But what is unusual is what she was wearing . . .

(ARCHIE *holds out his hand.* ANNA *heaves across the open book.*)

A leather bathing costume.

(EILEEN *is about to protest, when* ARCHIE *jabs viciously at the book with his finger.*)

It says here.

(ANNA *smiles.*) A leather bathing costume. And him standing with a hosepipe in his hand. (*A pause. He closes his eyes.*) Well, well, you ask why does she consent? It doesn't sound like pleasure in the ordinary sense of the word. It is not. It is corruption. In return for her performance the Burgomaster is using his influence to secure her a supply of fresh fruit and vegetables which she will sell at inflated prices. While our countrymen are dying on the Russian front, she will exploit their families at home. And meanwhile even as they romp, above the obscene display there sits an old woman locked in her room. The Burgomaster's wife. (*His coup de grâce.*) Alone. Listening. And blind.

52. INT. EILEEN'S ROOM. NIGHT

An identical room to ANNA's *but* EILEEN *has made it more homely with photographs and a dressing table stacked with make-up.* EILEEN *is sitting at it in her slip, getting ready for dinner.* ANNA *stands behind her, already dressed. They are laughing.*

EILEEN: He is going mad.

ANNA: D'you think so?

EILEEN: I'm sure. He is barking mad.

(*They both laugh.* EILEEN *looks at herself in the mirror intently. Then at* ANNA *pacing behind her.*)

Are you having a thing with him?

ANNA: I suppose so. I suppose that's what a thing is. (*A pause.* EILEEN *smiles.*)

EILEEN: What does he really think about . . . ?

ANNA: I don't know. I don't know what he thinks about
anything. We've never had a conversation. We just have a
thing.
(*She looks down at* EILEEN. *Then bursts out laughing.*) Isn't life
wonderful?

53. INT. HALL. NIGHT
The Unit going in to dinner. ANNA *and* EILEEN *come down the stairs
together.* LANGLEY *is standing outside his office as they come down. He
moves across to intercept them.*
LANGLEY: Eileen. There's somebody to see you.
EILEEN: Oh, really?
LANGLEY: Would you like to use my room?
      (EILEEN *goes in.* LANGLEY *closes the door behind her but we just
      glimpse a* UNIFORMED OFFICER *as the door shuts.* ANNA *is left
      standing looking across at* LANGLEY.)
Her brother has been killed. Singapore.
      (ANNA *stands completely stunned by the news.* LANGLEY *watches.
      Then she speaks quietly.*)
ANNA: Oh God . . .

54. INT. EILEEN'S ROOM. NIGHT
ANNA *and* EILEEN *in each other's arms rocking backwards and forwards.*
EILEEN *is hysterical with grief, wild, out of control, like a drowning
woman. The make-up has scarred her face. She is screaming.*
EILEEN: All the time . . .
ANNA: Yes, I know . . .
EILEEN: All the time . . .
ANNA: I know.
EILEEN: All the time we've been here . . .
ANNA: Yes.
EILEEN: All the time, all the time we've been here.
ANNA: Yes, I know.
EILEEN: I can't stand it. I can't stand it.
ANNA: No.
EILEEN: I can't stand what we've done.

55. INT. HALL. NIGHT

In the darkness a single shaft of light falls on EILEEN's *cases stacked by the door. The* OFFICER *we have glimpsed comes across and picks up her coat which is draped across them. Then* EILEEN *comes into frame, still crying gently. He puts the coat round her shoulders, picks up her handbag. Then leans across her and whispers quietly. The tiny scuffles of grief.* ANNA *watches in an upstairs doorway.*

56. INT. GUN ROOM. NIGHT

ANNA *enters the darkened room with a cup of tea.* ARCHIE *is standing staring at the blacked-out window, his back to the door.*

ANNA: Do you want this?

ARCHIE: Just put it down.

(ANNA *crosses to the desk and puts tea on it.*)

ARCHIE: What time is it?

ANNA: Two.

ARCHIE: Has she gone?

ANNA: Mmm-mm. (*Pause.*) You should have said goodbye to her.

ARCHIE: What?

ANNA: That was the decent thing to do.

(ARCHIE *turns and moves towards the desk.*)

ARCHIE: There's a broadcast here I've just completed. I want it transmitted as fast as possible. You'll also have to take on Eileen's secretarial tasks. Get right down to it in the morning, will you?

ANNA: No, I won't.

(*Pause.* ARCHIE *looks at* ANNA.)

ARCHIE: I set maself the task. Get through the war. Just get through it, that's all. Put it no higher than that. Accept it. Endure it. But don't think, because if you begin to think, it'll all come apart in your hands. So. Let's all have the time of our lives not bothering to think about a bloody thing. Just . . . get on with it. This house is the war. And I'd rather be anywhere, I'd rather be in France, I'd rather be in the desert, I'd rather be in a Wellington over Berlin, anywhere but here with you and your people in this bloody awful English house . . . but I shall spend it here.

121

(*Pause.*)

ANNA: Strange thing; as if to suffer and say nothing were clever.
As if to do this degrading work were clever. As if that were
clever.

(*Long pause.*) Will you hold me? Will you touch me?

ARCHIE: No.

(*He looks down.*)

57. INT. BEDROOM. NIGHT

ANNA *sits dressed on her bed reading* ARCHIE's *script. We look at the
pages. They are a mass of scrawled instructions and underlinings. There
are Stars of David scratched in bright red ink, there are exclamation marks
and enormous phrases like 'Now look here', and 'Stress this'. Some phrases
refer to disease and corruption. We look at* ANNA *again. She regularly puts
the sheets aside. Her face is dead.*

58. INT. LANGLEY'S OFFICE. DAY

LANGLEY *working at his desk, looks up.* ANNA *standing at the door.
Bright morning light.*

ANNA: There's a broadcast here. I'm not sure it's quite right.

LANGLEY: Come in.

(ANNA *comes in and sits down opposite him at the desk.*)
Tell me about it.

ANNA: Well . . . apparently one of Goebbels's newspapers has
singled out for special praise the work of some doctors on
the Russian front who run blood transfusion units and
who've been successful in saving many, many lives.

LANGLEY: Yes.

ANNA: Now our idea in reply is to say that the units are getting
their supplies of blood not from good clean fellow Germans,
but from Polish and Russian prisoners who have not even
had a Wassermann test. In other words, our job is to
convince an army which we believe has just sustained the
most appalling losses in the history of human warfare that
those of them who have managed to escape death are on
the point of being consumed with veneral disease.

(*There is a pause.* LANGLEY *spreads his hands.*)

LANGLEY: It sounds a very good idea.

ANNA: You don't think he's mad? You don't think, clinically, Archie Maclean is mad?

(*Pause.*)

LANGLEY: We don't really know what's happening on the Russian front. But people are telling us that one million Germans have died in Russia in the last eight months. And of those maybe half have been killed in battle. The rest have just curled up in their greatcoats and died. Of frostbite. Exposure. Well nobody in that party went of their own accord. They went because they were inspired to go. By that great genius Joseph Goebbels. And they stayed, in part, because of the work he is doing. And because of that work, they are still there. And they are still dying. Now if you want to tell me that you can't draft that broadcast, then you had best return to your country estate, because we have as much duty to assist our side as he has his. And we must bring to it the same vigour, the same passion, the same intelligence that he has brought to his. And if this involves throwing a great trail of aniseed across Europe, if it means covering the whole continent in obloquy and filth . . . then that is what we shall do. (*A pause.* ANNA *quite lost.* LANGLEY *looks across at her.*)

There has been a complaint about you. From Maclean. He spoke to me this morning. Your German is good and so is your application. But he feels from the start you have tried to compromise him. I put it another way. You have tried unsuccessfully to get him to sleep with you. Please. There is the question of legality—your age. Also Maclean knows something of your background, your family, how little you know of the world, and felt to take advantage would be indefensible. And he has come to feel that the pressure is now intolerable and rather than have to upset you in person, he has asked me to request you to resign.

ANNA: But it's not true.

LANGLEY: I don't care if it's true. You have unbalanced one of our most gifted writers. That is unforgivable.

(*A pause.* LANGLEY *takes out a clean piece of stationery from his desk drawer and pushes it across the desk with a fountain pen.*)
A letter of resignation.

ANNA: No.

LANGLEY: Otherwise I shall have to speak to your father, tell him what's occurred.

ANNA: But it's not true, it's not what happened. None of it's true.

LANGLEY: Then why did he say it?
(*Silence. We look at* ANNA.)

ANNA: No.

59. BLANK SCREEN

VOICE: Five months later, in July 1942, Otto Abend Eins made his final broadcast.

60. INT. BILLIARD ROOM. NIGHT

The Unit gathered round the table, minus ANNA, EILEEN *and* ARCHIE. *But* FENNEL *is present this time, watching from the side.* KARL *is in full flood.* JUNGKE *is listening.*

KARL: Die deutsche Wehrmacht muss härter kämpfen, muss den Krieg mit einer Rücksichtslosigkeit führen, die sie bisher nicht gezeigt hat. Dieser Defaitismus frisst den Willen der deutschen Nation auf.
(LANGLEY *cues* LOTTERBY, *who then bangs his rifle butt against the inside of the door very loudly, so loudly the door almost splinters. Then the door is thrown open from the other side and* ARCHIE *is revealed standing with a machine-gun. He runs into the room and jumps on top of the billiard table.*)
Um Gotteswillen!

ARCHIE: Also. Otto. Wir haben ihn gefunden.
(*He points the machine-gun at* KARL.)

KARL: Nein, nein! Bitte! Nicht!
(LANGLEY *cues again.* ARCHIE *fires the machine-gun deafeningly loud.* KARL *reels back clutching himself and moaning. His chair goes over and he falls to the floor.*)

ARCHIE: Also . . .

(ARCHIE *strides to the wireless equipment and in a huge gesture rips the cables out. Moves to stand over.*)

Otto ist tot.

(*With a creak* KARL *sits up from his dead position. His face breaks into a huge grin.*)

61. EXT. HOUSE. DAY

The house seen from the outside. Its main doors are opened and out from it come the SOLDIERS *and their* SERGEANT *carrying out office and wireless equipment.* FENNEL, *with his* NAVAL COMMANDER, *follows them and gets into his car.* LANGLEY *shakes his hand.*

VOICE: The work of the department continued until the end of the war when all its official records were destroyed. Many of the most brilliant men from the Propaganda and Intelligence Services went on to careers in public life, in Parliament, Fleet Street, the universities and the BBC.

62. EXT. COUNCIL ESTATE. DAY

FENNEL *moves in an election van, speaking on the back of a jeep which is plastered with photos of himself and the slogan 'Let's Go With Labour'.*

VOICE: John Fennel resumed a career in politics which took him in 1968 to a Cabinet rank which he lost with Labour's subsequent defeat in 1970.

63. EXT. NURSING HOME. DAY

LANGLEY *in his bathchair being wheeled across a lawn by an obviously expensive* PRIVATE NURSE. *He looks ill and drawn.*

VOICE: Will Langley went on to become a world-famous thriller writer in the mid-fifties. His work helped to establish a genre notable for its sustained passages of sexuality and violence. He died in 1962.

64. EXT. GOLF COURSE. DAY

Amateur film. The sound of a projector. EILEEN GRAHAM *on the golf course, looking much older, in a sensible skirt and windcheater. She fools around for the camera.*

VOICE: Eileen Graham started a chain of employment agencies

specializing in temporary secretaries. She is President of the
Guild of British Businesswomen. She has never married.

65. INT. VIEWING THEATRE. NIGHT

ARCHIE MACLEAN *viewing rushes. He is sitting forward, the beam of the
projector behind his shoulder.*

VOICE: Archie Maclean was transferred that year to the Crown
Film Unit, where he made distinguished documentaries. He
became known in the fifties for his award-winning feature
films . . .

66. INT. SLUM HOUSE. DAY

A sequence from ARCHIE's *black-and-white film, made in the late fifties.
A small boy watches as his father is washed in a tin bath by his mother.*

VOICE: . . . which he both wrote and directed. The most famous
example is *A Kind of Life*, a loving and lyrical evocation of
his own childhood in Glasgow. But his most recent work
starring some of Hollywood's best loved names . . .

67. EXT. SEA. DAY

A sequence from one of ARCHIE's *latest films. A runaway car speeds off
the end of a pier and crashes into the water.*

VOICE: . . . has commanded little of the same critical attention or
respect.

68. BLANK SCREEN

VOICE: Anna Seaton.

69. STILLS SEQUENCE

ANNA *in a sequence of black-and-white stills is seen in an advertising
agency leaning over an artist's shoulder to look at a drawing of a comic
dog.*

VOICE: Entered advertising in 1946 where she remained for ten
years, increasingly distressed at the compromises forced on
her by her profession. In 1956 she resigned and announced
her intention to live an honest life.

70. STILLS SEQUENCE
A semi-detached in Fulham, seen from outside.
VOICE: She told her husband she was having an affair with
    another man, and could no longer bear the untruths of
    adultery. Her husband left her.

71. STILLS SEQUENCE
A brightly lit hospital seen from outside.
VOICE: After a period of lavish promiscuity she suffered an
    infected womb and an enforced hysterectomy.

72. STILLS SEQUENCE
Grosvenor Square demonstrations, 1968.
VOICE: She became a full-time researcher for the Labour Party,
    until she left during the Vietnam demonstrations and went
    to live with a young unmarried mother in Wales.

73. STILLS SEQUENCE
ANNA, *much older, playing on a Welsh hillside with a small girl and a*
dog.
VOICE: Having travelled to see Maclean's latest film at a seaside
    Odeon, she was driven to write to him for the first time
    since 1942, complaining of the falseness of his films, the
    way they sentimentalized what she knew to be his appalling
    childhood and lamenting, in sum, the films' lack of political
    direction. The last paragraph of her letter read:

74. INT. HOUSE. DAY
Shots of the empty rooms inside the house after the Unit has gone.
Dining-room. Drawing-room. Bedroom. Gun room. All empty, standing
deserted.
ANNA: (VO) It is only now that I fully understand the events
    that passed between us so many years ago. You must allow
    for my ignorance, I was born into a class and at a time that
    protected me from even a chance acquaintance with the
    world. But since that first day at Wendlesham I have been
    trying to learn, trying to keep faith with the shame and

anger I saw in you. In retrospect what you sensed then has become blindingly clear to the rest of us: that whereas we knew exactly what we were fighting against, none of us had the whisper of an idea as to what we were fighting for. Over the years I have been watching the steady impoverishment of the people's ideals, their loss of faith, the lying, the daily inveterate lying, the thirty-year-old deep corrosive national habit of lying, and I have remembered you. I have remembered the one lie you told to make me go away. And I now at last have come to understand why you told it. I loved you then and I love you now. For thirty years you have been the beat of my heart. Please, please tell me it is the same for you.

75. EXT. HOUSE. DAY
The house seen from outside.
VOICE: He never replied.
    (*The house sits in the sun. A few seconds, then:*)

76. END CREDITS
Chopin's Waltz No. 3 in A Minor.

Plenty

For Kate

Characters

SUSAN TRAHERNE

ALICE PARK

RAYMOND BROCK

CODENAME LAZAR

A FRENCHMAN

LEONARD DARWIN

MICK

LOUISE

M AUNG

MME AUNG

DORCAS FREY

JOHN BEGLEY

SIR ANDREW CHARLESON

ANOTHER FRENCHMAN

Plenty was first performed at the Lyttelton Theatre on 7 April 1978. The cast was as follows:

SUSAN TRAHERNE	Kate Nelligan
ALICE PARK	Julie Covington
RAYMOND BROCK	Stephen Moore
CODENAME LAZAR	Paul Freeman
A FRENCHMAN	Robert Ralph
SIR LEONARD DARWIN	Basil Henson
MICK	David Schofield
LOUISE	Gil Brailey
M AUNG	Kristopher Kum
MME AUNG	Me Me Lai
DORCAS FREY	Lindsay Duncan
JOHN BEGLEY	Tom Durham
SIR ANDREW CHARLESON	Frederick Treves
ANOTHER FRENCHMAN	Timothy Davies
Director	David Hare
Settings	Hayden Griffin
Costumes	Deirdre Clancy
Music	Nick Bicât

Plenty

SCENE I

Knightsbridge. Easter 1962.

A wooden floor. At the back of the stage high windows give the impression of a room which has been stripped bare. Around the floor are packing cases full of fine objects. At the front lies a single mattress, on which a naked man is sleeping face downwards.

SUSAN *sits on one of the packing cases. In her middle thirties, she is thin and well presented. She wastes no energy. She now rolls an Old Holborn and lights it.*

ALICE *comes in from the street, a blanket over her head. She carries a small tinfoil parcel. She is small-featured, slightly younger and busier than* SUSAN. *She wears jeans. She drops the blanket and shakes the rain off herself.*

ALICE: I don't know why anybody lives in this country. No
  wonder everyone has colds all the time. Even what they call
  passion, it still comes at you down a blocked nose.
  (SUSAN *smokes quietly.* ALICE *is distracted by some stray object
  which she tosses into a packing case. The man stirs and turns over.
  He is middle-aged, running to fat and covered in dried blood.* SUSAN
  cues ALICE.)
SUSAN: And the food.
ALICE: Yeah. The wet. The cold. The flu. The food. The loveless
  English. How is he?
SUSAN: Fine.
  (ALICE *kneels down beside him.*)
ALICE: The blood is spectacular.
SUSAN: The blood is from his thumb.
  (ALICE *takes his penis between her thumb and forefinger.*)
ALICE: Turkey neck and turkey gristle, isn't that what they say?
  (*A pause.* SUSAN *smokes.*)
  Are you sure he's OK?
SUSAN: He had a couple of Nembutal and twelve fingers of

133

Scotch. It's nothing else, don't worry.

ALICE: And a fight.

SUSAN: A short fight.

(ALICE *takes the tinfoil parcel and opens it. Steam rises.*)

ALICE: Chinese takeaway. Want some?

SUSAN: It's six o'clock in the morning.

ALICE: Sweet and sour prawn.

SUSAN: No thanks.

ALICE: You should. You worked as hard as I did. When we
started last night, I didn't think it could be done.

(ALICE *gestures round the empty room. Then eats.* SUSAN *watches,
then gets up and stands behind her with a key.*)

SUSAN: It's a Yale. There's a mortise as well but I've lost the
key. There's a cleaning lady next door, should you want
one, her work's good but don't try talking about the blacks.
You have a share in that garden in the centre of the square,
you know all those trees and flowers they keep locked up.
The milkman calls daily, again he's nice, but don't touch
the yoghurt, it's green, we call it Venusian sperm.

(*Pause.*)

Good luck with your girls.

(SUSAN *turns to go.* ALICE *gets up.*)

ALICE: Are you sure you can't stay? I think you'd like them.

SUSAN: Unmarried mothers, I don't think I'd get on.

ALICE: I'm going to ring round at nine o'clock. If you just stayed
on for a couple of hours . . .

SUSAN: You don't really want that, nobody would.

(*Pause.*)

You must tell my husband . . .

ALICE: You've given me the house, and you went on your way.

SUSAN: Tell him I left with nothing that was his. I just walked
out on him. Everything to go.

(SUSAN *smiles again and goes out. There is a pause. The man stirs
again at the front of the stage.* ALICE *stands still holding the sweet
and sour prawn.*)

BROCK: Darling.

(BROCK *is still asleep. His eyes don't open as he turns over.* ALICE

watches very beadily. There is a long pause. Then he murmurs:)
What's for breakfast?
ALICE: Fish.

SCENE 2

St Benoît. November 1943.
    Darkness. From the dark the sound of the wireless. From offstage a beam of light flashes irregularly, cutting up through the night. Then back to dark.

ANNOUNCER: Ici Londres. Les voix de la liberté. Ensuite quelques messages personnels. Mon Oncle Albert a perdu son chien. Mon—Oncle—Albert—a—perdu—son—chien.
    (*A heavy thump in the darkness. Then the sound of someone running towards the noise. A small amount of light shows us the scene. LAZAR is trying to disentangle himself from his parachute. He has landed at the edge of the wood. At the back SUSAN runs on from a great distance, wrapped in a greatcoat against the cold. She has a scarf round her face so that only her eyes can be seen. She is extremely nervous and vulnerable, and her uncertainty makes her rude and abrupt.*)
SUSAN: Eh, qu'est-ce que vous faites ici?
LAZAR: Ah rien. Laisse-moi un moment, je peux tout expliquer.
    (SUSAN *takes a revolver from her pocket and moves towards him. She stoops down, feels the edge of* LAZAR's *parachute.*)
SUSAN: Donnez-moi votre sac.
    (LAZAR *throws across the satchel which has been tied to his waist.* SUSAN *looks through it, then puts the gun back in her pocket.*)
And your French is not good.
    (SUSAN *moves quickly away to listen for sounds in the night.* LAZAR *watches then speaks quietly to her back.* LAZAR *is a code name; he is, of course, English.*)
LAZAR: Where am I?
SUSAN: Please be quiet. I can't hear when you speak. (*Pause.*)

135

There's a road. Through the wood. Gestapo patrol.

LAZAR: I see.

SUSAN: I thought I heard something.

LAZAR: Are you waiting for supplies?

SUSAN: On the hour. There's meant to be a drop. I thought it was early, that's why I flashed.

LAZAR: I'm sorry. We had to take advantage of your light. We were losing fuel. I'm afraid I'm meant to be eighty miles on. Can you . . . could you tell me where I am?

SUSAN: You've landed near a village called St Benoît. It's close to a town called Poitiers, all right?

LAZAR: Yes. I think. I have heard of it you know.
(*Pause. She half turns but still does not look at him.*)

SUSAN: Hadn't you better take that thing off?

LAZAR: We are in the same racket, I suppose?

SUSAN: Well we're pretty well dished if we aren't. Did you spot any movement as you came down?

LAZAR: None at all. We just picked out your light.

SUSAN: If you didn't see anything I'd like to hold on. We need the drop badly—explosives and guns.

LAZAR: Have you come out on your own?
(*A pause. He has taken off his jump-suit. Underneath he is dressed as a French peasant. Now he puts a beret on.*)
You'd better tell me, how does this look?

SUSAN: I'd rather not look at you. It's an element of risk which we really don't need to take. In my experience it is best, it really is best if you always obey the rules.

LAZAR: But you'd like me to hold on and help you I think?
(*Pause.*)
Listen I'm happy I might be of some use. My own undertaking is somewhat up the spout. Whatever happens I'm several days late. If I could hold on and be of any help . . . I'm sure I'd never have to look you in the face.

SUSAN: All right, if you could just . . .

LAZAR: Look the opposite . . . yes. I will. I'm delighted.
(*He does so.*)
All right?

SUSAN: If you could hold on, I'm sure I could find you a bike.

LAZAR: Would you like a cigarette?

SUSAN: Thank you very much.

(*Pause.*)

Cafés are bad meeting places, much less safe than they seem. Don't go near Bourges, it's very bad for us. Don't carry anything in toothpaste tubes, it's become the first place they look. Don't laugh too much. An Englishman's laugh, it just doesn't sound the same. Are they still teaching you to broadcast from the lavatory?

LAZAR: Yes.

SUSAN: Well don't. And don't hide your receiver in the cistern, the whole dodge is badly out of date. The Gestapo have been crashing into lavatories for a full two months. Never take the valley road beyond Poitiers, I'll show you a side-road.

(*Pause.*)

And that's it really. The rest you know, or will learn.

LAZAR: How long have you been here?

SUSAN: Perhaps a year. Off and on. How's everyone at home?

LAZAR: They're fine.

SUSAN: The boss?

LAZAR: Fine. Gave me some cufflinks at the aerodrome. Told me my chances.

SUSAN: Fifty-fifty?

LAZAR: Yes.

SUSAN: He's getting out of touch.

(*Pause.*)

LAZAR: How has it been?

SUSAN: Well . . . the Germans are still here.

LAZAR: You mean we're failing?

SUSAN: Not at all. It's part of our brief. Keep them here, keep them occupied. Blow up their bridges, devastate the roads, so they have to waste their manpower chasing after us. Divert them from the front. Well that's what we've done.

LAZAR: I see.

SUSAN: But it's the worst thing about the job, the more successful

137

you are, the longer it goes on.

LAZAR: Until we win.

SUSAN: Oh yes.

(*Pause.*)

A friend . . . a friend who was here used to say, never kill a German, always shoot him in the leg. That way he goes to hospital where he has to be looked after, where he'll use up enemy resources. But a dead soldier is forgotten and replaced.

(*Pause.*)

LAZAR: Do you have dark hair?

SUSAN: What?

LAZAR: One strand across your face. Very young. Sitting one day next to the mahogany door. At the recruitment place. And above your shoulder at the other side, *Whitaker's Almanack*.

(SUSAN *turns.*)

SUSAN: You know who I am.

(*The sound of an aeroplane.* SUSAN *moves back and begins to flash her torch up into the night.* LAZAR *crosses.*)

LAZAR: That's it over there.

SUSAN: Wait.

LAZAR: Isn't that it?

SUSAN: Don't move across. Just wait.

LAZAR: That's the drop.

(*The light stops. And the sound of the plane dies.* SUSAN *moves back silently and stands behind* LAZAR *looking out into the field.*)

SUSAN: It's all right, leave it. It's safer to wait a moment or two.

LAZAR: Oh my God.

SUSAN: What?

LAZAR: Out across the field. Look . . .

SUSAN: Get down.

(*They both lie down.*)

LAZAR: He's picking it up. Let's get away from here.

SUSAN: No.

LAZAR: Come on, for God's sake . . .

SUSAN: No.

LAZAR: If it's the Gestapo . . .

SUSAN: Gestapo nothing, it's the bloody French.

(*From where they have been looking comes a dark figure running like mad with an enormous parcel wrapped in a parachute.* SUSAN *tries to intercept him. A furious row breaks out in heavy whispers.*)

Posez ça par terre, ce n'est pas à vous.

FRENCHMAN: Si, c'est à nous. Je ne vous connais pas.

SUSAN: Non, l'avion était anglais. C'est à nous.

FRENCHMAN: Non, c'est désigné pour la résistance.

LAZAR: Oh God.

(*He stands watching as* SUSAN, *handling the* FRENCHMAN *very badly, begins to lose her temper. They stand shouting in the night.*)

SUSAN: Vous savez bien que c'est nous qui devons diriger le mouvement de tous les armements. Pour les Français c'est tout à fait impossible . . .

FRENCHMAN: Va te faire foutre.

SUSAN: Si vous ne me le donnez pas . . .

FRENCHMAN: Les Anglais n'ont jamais compris la France. Il faut absolument que ce soit les Français qui déterminent notre avenir.

SUSAN: Posez ça . . .

FRENCHMAN: C'est pour la France.

(*The* FRENCHMAN *begins to go.* LAZAR *has walked quietly across to behind* SUSAN *and now takes the gun from her pocket. The* FRENCHMAN *sees it.*)

FRENCHMAN: Arr yew raven mad?

LAZAR: Please put it down.

(*Pause.*)

Please.

(*The* FRENCHMAN *lowers the package to the ground. Then stands up.*)

Please tell your friends we're sorry. We do want to help. Mais parfois ce sont les Français mêmes qui le rendent difficile.

FRENCHMAN: Nobody ask you. Nobody ask you to come. Vous n'êtes pas les bienvenus ici.

(SUSAN *about to reply but* LAZAR *holds up his hand at once.*)

139

LAZAR: Compris.

FRENCHMAN: Espèce de con.

> (*There is a pause. Then the* FRENCHMAN *turns and walks out.*
> LAZAR *keeps him covered, then turns to start picking the stuff up.*
> SUSAN *moves well away.*)

LAZAR: Bloody Gaullists.

> (*Pause.*)

I mean, what do they have for brains?

SUSAN: I don't know.

LAZAR: I mean really.

SUSAN: They just expect the English to die. They sit and watch us spitting blood in the streets.

> (LAZAR *looks up at* SUSAN, *catching her tone. Then moves towards her as calmly as he can.*)

LAZAR: Here's your gun.

> (LAZAR *slips the gun into* SUSAN's *pocket, but as he does she takes his hand into hers.*)

We must be off.

SUSAN: I'm sorry, I'm so frightened.

LAZAR: I must bury the silk.

SUSAN: I'm not an agent, I'm just a courier. I carry messages between certain circuits . . .

LAZAR: Please . . .

SUSAN: I came tonight, it's my first drop, there is literally nobody else, I can't tell you the mess in Poitiers . . .

LAZAR: Please.

SUSAN: My friend, the man I mentioned, he's been taken to Buchenwald. He was the wireless operator, please let me tell you, his name was Tony . . .

LAZAR: I can't help.

SUSAN: I have to talk . . .

LAZAR: No.

SUSAN: What's the point, what's the point of following the rules if . . . ?

LAZAR: You mustn't . . .

SUSAN: I don't want to die. I don't want to die like that.

> (*Suddenly* SUSAN *embraces* LAZAR, *putting her head on his shoulder*

and crying uncontrollably. He puts his hand through her hair.
Then after a long time, she turns and walks some paces away, in
silence. They stand for some time.)

LAZAR: Did you know . . . did you know sound waves never die?
So every noise we make goes into the sky. And there is a
place somewhere in the corner of the universe where all the
babble of the world is kept.
(*Pause. Then* LAZAR *starts gathering the equipment together.*)
Come on, let's clear this lot up. We must be off. I don't
know how I'm going to manage on French cigarettes. Is
there somewhere I can buy bicycle clips? I was thinking
about it all the way down. Oh yes and something else. A
mackerel sky. What is the phrase for that?

SUSAN: Un ciel pommelé.

LAZAR: Un ciel pommelé. Marvellous. I must find a place to slip
it in. Now. Where will I find this bike?
(LAZAR *has collected everything and gone out.* SUSAN *follows him.*)

SUSAN: I don't know your name.

SCENE 3

Brussels. June 1947.
From the dark the sound of a small string orchestra gives way to the
voice of an ANNOUNCER.

ANNOUNCER: Ici Bruxelles—INR. Et maintenant notre soirée
continue avec la musique de Victor Sylvester et son
orchestre. Victor Sylvester est parmi les musiciens anglais
les plus aimés à cause de ses maintes émissions à la radio
anglaise pendant la guerre.
(*Evening. A gilt room. A fine desk. Good leather chairs. A portrait*
of the King. Behind the desk SIR LEONARD DARWIN *is working,*
silver-haired, immaculate, well into his late forties. A knock at the
door and RAYMOND BROCK *comes in. An ingenuous figure, not yet*
thirty, with a small moustache and a natural energy he finds hard to
contain in the proper manner. He refers constantly to his superior and

141

this makes him uneasy.)

BROCK: Sir Leonard . . .

DARWIN: Come in.

BROCK: A few moments of your time. If I could possibly . . .

DARWIN: You have my ear.

BROCK: The case of a British national who's died. It's just been
landed in my lap. A tourist named Radley's dropped dead
in his hotel. It was a coronary, seems fairly clear. The
Belgian police took the matter in hand, but naturally the
widow has come along to us. It should be quite easy, she's
taking it well.

(DARWIN *nods.* BROCK *goes to the door.*)

BROCK: Mrs Radley. The ambassador.

(SUSAN *has come in. She is simply and soberly dressed. She looks
extremely attractive.*)

DARWIN: If you'd like to sit down.

(*She sits opposite him at the desk.* BROCK *stands respectfully at the
other side of the room.*)

Please accept my condolences. The Third Secretary has
told me a little of your plight. Naturally we'll help in any
way we can.

BROCK: I've already taken certain practical steps. I've been to
the mortuary.

SUSAN: That's very kind.

BROCK: Belgian undertakers.

DARWIN: One need not say more. Your husband had a heart
attack, is that right?

SUSAN: Yes. In the foyer of our hotel.

DARWIN: Painless . . .

SUSAN: I would hope. He was packing the car. We were planning
to move on this morning. We only have two weeks. We
were hoping to make Innsbruck, at least if our travel
allowance would last. It was our first holiday since the war.

DARWIN: Brock, a handkerchief.

SUSAN: No.

(*Pause.*)

BROCK: I was persuaded to opt for an embalming, I'm afraid. It may involve you in some small extra cost.

SUSAN: Excuse me, but you'll have to explain the point.

BROCK: Sorry?

SUSAN: Of the embalming I mean.

(BROCK *looks to his superior, but decides to persist*.)

BROCK: Well, particularly in the summer it avoids the possibility of the body exploding at a bad moment. I mean any moment would be bad, it goes without saying, but on the aeroplane, say.

SUSAN: I see.

BROCK: You see, normally you find the body's simply washed . . . I don't know how much detail you want me to provide . . .

DARWIN: I would think it better if . . .

SUSAN: No, I would like to know. Tony was a doctor. He would want me to know.

(BROCK *pauses, then speaks with genuine interest*.)

BROCK: To be honest I was surprised at how little there is to do. There's a small bottle of spirit, colourless, and they simply give the body a wash. The only other thing is the stomach, if there's been a meal, a recent meal . . .

SUSAN: Tony had . . .

BROCK: Yes, he had breakfast I think. You insert a pipe into the corpse's stomach to let the gases out. They insert it and there's a strange sort of sigh.

(DARWIN *shifts*.)

DARWIN: If, er . . .

BROCK: It leaves almost no mark. Apparently, so they told me, the morgue attendants when they're bored sometimes set light to the gas for a joke. Makes one hell of a bang.

DARWIN: Shall we all have a drink?

(DARWIN *gets up*. BROCK *tries to backtrack*.)

BROCK: But of course I'm sure it didn't happen in this particular case.

DARWIN: No. There is gin. There is tonic. Yes?

SUSAN: Thank you.

(DARWIN *mixes drinks and hands them round*.)

BROCK: I'm afraid we shall need to discuss the practical arrangements. I know the whole subject is very distressing but there is the question . . . you do want the body flown back?

SUSAN: Well, I can hardly stash it in the boot of the car.

(*A pause.* DARWIN *lost.*)

DARWIN: What the Third Secretary is saying . . . not buried on foreign soil.

SUSAN: No.

BROCK: Quite. You see for the moment we take care of it, freight charges, and His Majesty's Government picks up the bill. But perhaps later we will have to charge it to the estate, if there is an estate. I'm sorry, I don't mean to interfere . . .

SUSAN: I'm sure there'll be enough to pay for it all. Tony made a very reasonable living.

(DARWIN *gets up.*)

DARWIN: Well, I think we now understand your needs. I shall go downstairs and set the matter in train.

BROCK: Would you prefer it if I did that, sir?

DARWIN: No, no. You stay and talk to Mrs Radley. I'll have a word with the travel people, make a booking on tomorrow morning's flight, if that suits?

SUSAN: Yes, of course.

DARWIN: You will be going back with the body, I assume?

SUSAN: Yes.

DARWIN: Are there other dependants? Children?

SUSAN: No.

(DARWIN *goes out. A pause.*)

BROCK: If . . .

SUSAN: He doesn't like you.

BROCK: Sorry.

SUSAN: The ambassador.

BROCK: Oh. Well, no.

(*Pause.*)

I don't think he's over the moon about you.

SUSAN: I shouldn't have said that.

BROCK: No, it's just . . . Darwin thinks disasters are

examinations in etiquette. Which fork to use in an
earthquake.

SUSAN: Darwin, is that his name?

BROCK: Yes, the mission all thinks it's God's joke. God getting
his own back by dashing off a modern Darwin who is in
every aspect less advanced than the last. (*He smiles alone.*)
I'm sorry. We sit about in the evenings and polish our
jokes. Brussels is rather a debilitating town.

SUSAN: Is this a bad posting for you?

BROCK: I'd been hoping for something more positive. Fresher
air. The flag still flies over a quarter of the human race and
I would like to have seen it really. Whereas here . . . we're
left with the problems of the war . . . (*He smiles again.*) Have
you met any prison governors?

SUSAN: No.

BROCK: It's just they talk exactly like us. I was hoping for
Brixton but I got the Scrubs. Just the same.

SUSAN: Does nobody like it here?

BROCK: The misery is contagious, I suppose. You spend the day
driving between bomb sites, watching the hungry, the
homeless, the bereaved. We think there are thirty million
people loose in Europe who've had to flee across borders,
have had to start again. And it is very odd to watch it all
from here. (*He gestures round the room.*) Had you been
married long?

SUSAN: We met during the war.

BROCK: I did notice some marks on the body.

SUSAN: Tony was a wireless operator with SOE. Our job was
harassment behind the lines. Very successful in Holland,
Denmark. Less so in France. Tony was in a circuit the
Gestapo destroyed. Then scattered. Ravensbruk,
Buchenwald, Saarbrucken, Dachau. Some were tortured,
executed.

BROCK: What did you do?

SUSAN: I was a courier. I was never caught.

(*She looks straight at* BROCK.)

I wasn't his wife.

BROCK: No.

SUSAN: Had you realized that?

BROCK: I'd thought it possible.

(*Pause.*)

SUSAN: What about Darwin, did he realize?

BROCK: Lord, no, it would never occur to him.

SUSAN: Motoring together it was easier to say we were man and wife. In fact I was barely even his mistress. He simply rang me a few weeks ago and asked if I'd like a holiday abroad. I was amazed. People in our organization really didn't know each other all that well. You made it your business to know as little as possible, it was a point of principle. Even now you don't know who most of your colleagues were. Perhaps you were in it. Perhaps I met you. I don't know.

(*Pause.*)

Tony I knew a bit better, not much, but I was glad when he rang. Those of us who went through this kind of war, I think we do have something in common. It's a kind of impatience, we're rather intolerant, we don't suffer fools. And so we get rather restless back in England, the people who stayed behind seem childish and a little silly. I think that's why Tony needed to get away. If you haven't suffered . . . well. And so driving through Europe with Tony I knew that at least I'd be able to act as I pleased for a while. That's all.

(*Pause.*)

It's kind of you not to have told the ambassador.

BROCK: Perhaps I will. (*He smiles.*) May I ask a question?

SUSAN: Yes.

BROCK: If you're not his wife, did he have one?

SUSAN: Yes.

BROCK: I see.

SUSAN: And three children. I had to lie about those, I couldn't claim them somehow. She lives in Crediton in Devon. She believes that Tony was travelling alone. He'd told her he needed two weeks by himself. That's what I was hoping you could do for me.

BROCK: Ah.

SUSAN: Phone her. I've written the number down. I'm afraid I
did it before I came.

(SUSAN *opens her handbag and hands across a card.* BROCK *takes
it.*)

BROCK: And lie?

SUSAN: Yes. I'd prefer it if you lied. But it's up to you.

(*She looks at* BROCK. *He makes a nervous half-laugh.*)

All right, doesn't matter . . .

BROCK: That's not what I said.

SUSAN: Please, it doesn't matter.

(*Pause.*)

BROCK: When did you choose me?

SUSAN: What?

BROCK: For the job. You didn't choose Darwin.

SUSAN: I might have done.

(*Pause.*)

BROCK: You don't think you wear your suffering a little
heavily? This smart club of people you belong to who had a
very bad war . . .

SUSAN: All right.

BROCK: I mean I know it must have put you on a different level
from the rest of us . . .

SUSAN: You won't shame me, you know. There's no point.

(*Pause.*)

It was an innocent relationship. That doesn't mean
unphysical. Unphysical isn't innocent. Unphysical in my
view is repressed. It just means there was no guilt. I wasn't
particularly fond of Tony, he was very slow-moving and
egg-stained if you know what I mean, but we'd known
some sorrow together and I came with him. And so it
seemed a shocking injustice when he fell in the lobby,
unjust for him of course, but also unjust for me, alone, a
long way from home, and worst of all for his wife, bitterly
unfair if she had to have the news from me. Unfair for life.
And so I approached the embassy.

(*Pause.*)

Obviously I shouldn't even have mentioned the war. Tony
used to say don't talk about it. He had a dread of being
trapped in small rooms with big Jewesses, I know exactly
what he meant. I should have just come here this evening
and sat with my legs apart, pretended to be a scarlet
woman, then at least you would have been able to place
me. It makes no difference. Lie or don't lie. It's a matter of
indifference.

(BROCK *gets up and moves uncertainly around the room.* SUSAN *stays
where she is.*)

BROCK: Would you . . . perhaps I could ask you to dinner? Just
so we could talk . . .

SUSAN: No. I refuse to tell you anything now. If I told you
anything about myself you would just think I was pleading,
that I was trying to get round you. So I tell you nothing. I
just say look at me—don't creep round the furniture—look
at me and make a judgement.

BROCK: Well . . .

(DARWIN *reappears. He picks up his drink and sits at his desk as if
to clear up. There is in fact nothing to clear up, so mostly he just
moves his watch round. He talks the while.*)

DARWIN: That's done. First flight tomorrow without a hitch.

(BROCK *stands as if unaware* DARWIN *has come back.*)

SUSAN: Thank you very much.

DARWIN: If there's anything else. There is a small chapel in the
embassy if you'd like to use it before you go.

SUSAN: Thank you.

(BROCK *turns and walks abruptly out of the room.* SUSAN *smiles a
moment.* DARWIN *puts on his watch.*)

Have you been posted here long?

DARWIN: No, not at all. Just a few months. Before that,
Djakarta. We were hoping for something sunny but
Brussels came along. Not that we're complaining. They've
certainly got something going here.

SUSAN: Really?

DARWIN: Oh yes. New Europe. Yes yes.

(*Pause.*)

Reconstruction. Massive. Massive work of reconstruction.
Jobs. Ideals. Marvellous. Marvellous time to be alive in
Europe. No end of it. Roads to be built. People to be
educated. Land to be tilled. Lots to get on with.
(*Pause.*)
Have another gin.

SUSAN: No thanks.

DARWIN: The diplomat's eye is the clearest in the world. Seen
from Djakarta this continent looks so old, so beautiful. We
don't realize what we have in our hands.

SUSAN: No.

(BROCK *reappears at the door.*)

BROCK: Your wife is asking if you're ready for dinner, sir.

DARWIN: Right.

BROCK: And she wants your advice on her face.

(DARWIN *gets up.*)

I'll lock up after you, sir.

DARWIN: You'll see Mrs Radley to her hotel?

BROCK: Of course.

DARWIN: Goodbye, Mrs Radley. I'm sorry it hasn't been a
happier day.

(DARWIN *goes out.* BROCK *closes the door. He looks at* SUSAN.)

BROCK: I've put in a call to England. There's an hour's delay.

(*Pause.*)

I've decided to lie.

(BROCK *and* SUSAN *stare at each other. Silence.*)

Will you be going back with the body?

SUSAN: No.

(BROCK *goes to the door and listens. Then turns back and removes
the buttonhole. He looks for somewhere to put it. He finds his
undrunk gin and tonic and puts it in there. Then he takes his jacket
off and drops it somewhat deliberately on the floor. He takes a couple
of paces towards* SUSAN.)

BROCK: Will you remind me to cancel your seat?

Scene 4

Pimlico. September 1947.

From the dark the sound of a string quartet. It comes to an end. Then a voice.

ANNOUNCER: This is the BBC Third Programme. Vorichef wrote *Les Ossifiés* in the year of the Paris Commune, but his struggle with Parkinson's disease during the writing of the score has hitherto made it a peculiarly difficult manuscript for musicologists to interpret. However the leader of the Bremen Ensemble has recently done a magnificent work of reclamation. Vorichef died in an extreme state of senile dementia in 1878. This performance of his last work will be followed by a short talk in our series 'Musicians and Disease'. (*A bed-sitter with some wooden chairs, a bed and a canvas bed with a suitcase set beside it. A small room, well maintained but cheerless.* ALICE *sits on the floor in a chalk-striped men's suit and white tie. She smokes a hookah.* SUSAN *is on the edge of the bed drinking cocoa. She is wearing a blue striped shirt. Her revolver lies beside her.* BROCK *is laid out fast asleep across two chairs in his pinstripes. Next to him is a large pink parcel, an odd item of luxury in the dismal surroundings. By the way they talk you know it's late.*)

SUSAN: I want to move on. I do desperately want to feel I'm moving on.

ALICE: With him?

SUSAN: Well that's the problem, isn't it?

(*Pause.* ALICE *smiles.*)

ALICE: You are strange.

SUSAN: Well, what would you do?

ALICE: I'd trade him in.

SUSAN: Would you?

ALICE: I'd choose someone else off the street.

SUSAN: And what chance would you have tonight, within a mile, say, within a mile of here?

ALICE: Let me think. Does that take in Victoria Coach Station?

SUSAN: No.

ALICE: Then pretty slim.

SUSAN: Is that right?

(*They smile. The hookah smokes.*)

That thing is disgusting.

ALICE: I know. It was better when the dung was fresh.

SUSAN: I don't know why you bother . . .

ALICE: The writer must experience everything, every kind of degradation. Nothing is closed to him. It's really the degradation that attracted me to the job.

SUSAN: I thought you were going to work tonight . . .

ALICE: I can't write all the time. You have to live it before you can write it. What other way is there? Besides nicking it.

SUSAN: Is that done?

ALICE: Apparently. Once you start looking it seems most books are copied out of other books. Only it's called tribute. Tribute to Hemingway. Means it's nicked. Mine's going to be tribute to Scott Fitzgerald. Have you read him?

SUSAN: No.

ALICE: *Last Tycoon.* Mine's going to be like that. Not quite the same of course. Something of a bitch to make Ealing Broadway hum like Hollywood Boulevard but otherwise it's in the bag.

(BROCK *grunts.*)

He snores.

SUSAN: You should get a job.

ALICE: I've had a job, I know what jobs are like. Had a job in your office.

SUSAN: For three days.

ALICE: It was enough.

SUSAN: How are you going to live?

ALICE: Off you mostly. (*She smiles.*) Susan . . .

SUSAN: I want to move on. I do desperately want to feel I'm moving on.

(*Pause.*)

I work so hard I have no time to think. The office is worse.
Those brown invoices go back and forth, import, export . . .

ALICE: I remember.

SUSAN: They get heavier and heavier as the day goes on, I can
barely stagger across the room for the weight of a single
piece of paper, by the end of the day if you dropped one on
the floor, you would smash your foot. The silence is worse.
Dust gathering. Water lapping beyond the wall. It seems
unreal. You can't believe that because of the work you do
ships pass and sail across the world. (*She stares a moment.*)
Mr Medlicott has moved into my office.

ALICE: Frightful Mr Medlicott?

SUSAN: Yes.

ALICE: The boss?

SUSAN: He has moved in. Or rather, more sinister still he has
removed the frosted glass between our two offices.

ALICE: Really?

SUSAN: I came in one morning and found the partition had gone.
I interpret it as the first step in a mating dance. I believe
Medlicott stayed behind one night, set his ledger aside,
ripped off his tweed suit and his high collar, stripped
naked, took up an axe, swung it at the partition, dropped to
the floor, rolled over in the broken glass till he bled, till his
whole body streamed blood, then he cleared up, slipped
home, came back next morning and waited to see if
anything woud be said. But I have said nothing. And
neither has he. He puts his head down and does not lift it
till lunch. I have to look across at his few strands of hair,
like seaweed across his skull. And I am frightened of what
the next step will be.

ALICE: I can imagine.

SUSAN: The sexual pressure is becoming intolerable.

(*They smile.*)

One day there was a condom in his turn-up. Used or
unused I couldn't say. But planted without a doubt. Again,
nothing said. I tried to laugh it off to myself, pretended

he'd been off with some whore in Limehouse and not bothered to take his trousers off, so that after the event the condom had just absent-mindedly fallen from its place and lodged alongside all the bus tickets and the tobacco and the Smarties and the paper-clips and all the rest of it. But I know the truth. It was step two. And the dance has barely begun.

(*Pause.*)

Alice. I must get out.

ALICE: Then do. Just go. Have you never done that? I do it all the time.

SUSAN: They do need me in that place.

ALICE: So much the better, gives it much more point. That's always the disappointment when I leave, I always go before people even notice I've come. But you . . . you could really make a splash.

(BROCK *stirs*.)

He stirs.

SUSAN: I'd like to change everything but I don't know how.

(*She leans under her bed, pulls out a shoebox, starts to oil and clean her gun.*)

ALICE: Are you really fond of him?

SUSAN: You don't see him at his best. We had a week in Brussels which we both enjoyed. Now he comes over for the weekend whenever he can. But he tends to be rather sick on the boat.

ALICE: You should meet someone younger.

SUSAN: That's not what I mean. And I don't really like young men. You're through and out the other side in no time at all.

ALICE: I can introduce you . . .

SUSAN: I'm sure. I've only known you three weeks, but I've got the idea. Your flair for agonized young men. I think you get them in bulk from tuberculosis wards.

ALICE: I'm just catching up, that's all.

SUSAN: Of course.

ALICE: I was a late starter.

SUSAN: Oh yes, what are you, eighteen?

ALICE: I started late. Out of guilt. I had a protected childhood. Till I ran away. And very bad guilt. I was frightened to masturbate more than once a week, I thought my clitoris was like a torch battery, you know use it too much and it runs out.

(BROCK *wakes*.)

He wakes.

(*They watch as he comes round.*)

BROCK: What time is it?

ALICE: Raymond, can you give us your view? I was just comparing the efficiency of a well-known household object with . . .

SUSAN: Alice, leave him alone.

ALICE: It's getting on for five.

BROCK: I feel terrible.

SUSAN: (*Kissing his head*) I'll get you something to eat. Omelette all right? It's only powder, I'm afraid . . .

BROCK: Well . . .

SUSAN: Two spoons or three? And I'll sprinkle it with Milk of Magnesia. (*She goes out into the kitchen.*)

BROCK: It seems a bit pointless. It's only twelve hours till I'm back on the boat. (*He picks up the gun.*) Did I miss something?

ALICE: No. She's just fondling it.

BROCK: Ah.

(*He looks round.* ALICE *is watching him all the time.*)

I can't remember what . . .

ALICE: Music. On the wireless. You had us listening to some music.

BROCK: Ah that's right.

ALICE: Some composer who shook.

BROCK: I thought you'd have gone. Don't you have a flat?

ALICE: I did. But it had bad associations. I was disappointed in love.

BROCK: I see.

ALICE: And Susan said I could sleep here.

BROCK: (*Absently admiring her suit*) I must say I do think your clothes are very smart.

ALICE: Well I tell you he looks very good in mine. (*She nods at the parcel.*) Do you always bring her one of those?

BROCK: I certainly try to bring a gift if I can.

ALICE: You must have lots of money.

BROCK: Well, I suppose. I find it immoderately easy to acquire. I seem to have a sort of mathematical gift. The stock exchange. Money sticks to my fingers I find. I triple my income. What can I do?

ALICE: It must be very tiresome.

BROCK: Oh . . . I'm acclimatizing, you know. (*Smiles.*) I think everyone's going to be rich very soon. Once we've got over the effects of the war. It's going to be coming out of everyone's ears.

ALICE: Is that what you think?

BROCK: I'm absolutely sure. (*Pause.*) I do enjoy these weekends you know. Susan leads such an interesting life. Books. Conversation. People like you. The Foreign Office can make you feel pretty isolated—also, to be honest, make you feel pretty small, as if you're living on sufferance, you can imagine . . .

ALICE: Yes.

BROCK: Till I met Susan. The very day I met her, she showed me you must always do what you want. If you want something you must get it. I think that's a wonderful way to live don't you?

ALICE: I do. (*Pause. She smiles.*) Shall I tell you how my book begins?

BROCK: Well . . .

ALICE: There's a woman in a rape trial. And the story is true. The book begins at the moment where she has to tell the court what the accused has said to her on the night of the rape. And she finds she can't bring herself to say the words out loud. And so the judge suggests she writes them down on a piece of paper and it be handed round the court. Which she does. And it says, 'I want to have you. I must

have you now.' (*She smiles again.*) So they pass it round
the jury who all read it and pass it on. At the end of the
second row there's a woman jurist who's fallen asleep at the
boredom of the trial. So the man next to her has to nudge
her awake and hand her the slip of paper. She wakes up,
looks at it, then at him, smiles and puts it in her handbag.
(*She laughs.*) That woman is my heroine.

BROCK: Well, yes.

(SUSAN *returns, sets food on* BROCK*'s knee. Then returns to cleaning
her gun.* ALICE *tries to re-light her hookah.*)

SUSAN: Cheese omelette. What were you talking about?

ALICE: The rape trial.

SUSAN: Did you tell Raymond who the woman was?

BROCK: What do you mean?

SUSAN: I'm only joking, dear.

(ALICE *and* SUSAN *laugh.*)

BROCK: I'm not sure it's the sort of . . .

ALICE: Oh sod this stuff.

SUSAN: I said it was dung.

ALICE: I was promised visions.

BROCK: Well . . .

ALICE: It's because I'm the only bohemian in London. People
exploit me. Because there are no standards, you see. In
Paris or New York, there are plenty of bohemians, so the
kief is rich and sweet and plentiful but here . . . you'd be
better off to lick the gum from your ration card.

SUSAN: Perhaps Raymond will be posted to Morocco, bring some
back in his bag . . .

BROCK: I don't think that's really on.

SUSAN: Nobody would notice, from what you say. Nobody would
notice if you smoked it yourself.

ALICE: Are they not very sharp?

SUSAN: Not according to Raymond. The ones I've met are
buffoons . . .

BROCK: Susan, please . . .

SUSAN: Well it's you who call them buffoons.

BROCK: It's not quite what I say.

SUSAN: It's you who tells the stories. That man Darwin . . .

BROCK: Please . . .

SUSAN: How he needs three young men from public schools to strap him into his surgical support.

BROCK: I told you that in confidence.

SUSAN: In gloves.

ALICE: Really?

BROCK: Darwin is not a buffoon.

SUSAN: From your own lips . . .

BROCK: He just has slight problems of adjustment to the modern age.

SUSAN: You are laughing.

BROCK: I am not laughing.

SUSAN: There is a slight smile at the corner of your mouth . . .

BROCK: There is not. There is absolutely no smile.

SUSAN: Alice, I will paraphrase, let me paraphrase Raymond's view of his boss. I don't misrepresent you, dear, it is, in paraphrase, in sum, that he would not trust him to stick his prick into a bucket of lard.

(BROCK *puts his omelette to one side, uneaten.*)

Well, is he a joke or is he not?

BROCK: Certainly he's a joke.

SUSAN: Thank you.

BROCK: He's a joke between us. He is not a joke to the entire world.

(*A pause.* BROCK *looks at* ALICE. *Then he gets up.*)

I think I'd better be pushing off home.

(BROCK *goes and gets his coat. Puts it on.* SUSAN *at last speaks, very quietly.*)

SUSAN: And I wish you wouldn't use those words.

BROCK: What?

SUSAN: Words like 'push off home'. You're always saying it. 'Bit of a tight corner', 'one hell of a spot'. They don't belong.

BROCK: What do you mean?

SUSAN: They are not your words.

(*Pause.*)

BROCK: Well, I'm none too keen on your words either.

SUSAN: Oh yes, which?

BROCK: The words you've been using this evening.

SUSAN: Such as?

BROCK: You know perfectly well.

SUSAN: Such as, come on tell me, what words have I used?

BROCK: Words like . . .

(*Pause.*)

Bucket of lard.

(*Pause.*)

SUSAN: Alice, there is only the bath or the kitchen.

ALICE: I know.

(ALICE *goes out.* SUSAN *automatically picks up the omelette and starts to eat it.*)

BROCK: Are you going to let her live with you?

SUSAN: I like her. She makes me laugh.

(*Pause.*)

BROCK: I'm sorry, I was awful, I apologize. But the work I do is not entirely contemptible. Of course our people are dull, they're stuffy, they're death. But what other world do I have?

(*Pause.*)

SUSAN: I think of France more than I tell you. I was seventeen and I was thrown into the war. I often think of it.

BROCK: I'm sure.

SUSAN: The most unlikely people. People I met only for an hour or two. Astonishing kindnesses. Bravery. The fact you could meet someone for an hour or two and see the very best of them and then move on. Can you understand?

(*Pause.* BROCK *does not move.*)

For instance, there was a man in France. His code name was Lazar. I'd been there a year I suppose and one night I had to see him on his way. He just dropped out of the sky. An agent. He was lost. I was trying to be blasé, trying to be tough, all the usual stuff—irony, hardness, cleverness, wit—and then suddenly I began to cry. On to the shoulder of a man I'd never met before. But not a day goes by without my wondering where he is.

(SUSAN *finishes her omelette and puts the plate aside.* BROCK *moves towards her.*)

BROCK: Susan.

SUSAN: I think we should try a winter apart. I really do. I think it's all a bit easy this way. These weekends. Nothing is tested. I think a test would be good. Then we would know. And what better test than a winter apart?

BROCK: A winter together.

(*Pause. They smile.*)

SUSAN: I would love to come to Brussels, you know that. I would love to come if it weren't for my job. But the shipping office is very important to me. I do find it fulfilling. And I just couldn't let Mr Medlicott down.

(*Pause.*)

You must say what you think.

(BROCK *looks at* SUSAN *hard, then shrugs and smiles.*)

I know you've been dreading the winter crossings, high seas . . .

BROCK: Don't patronize me, Susan.

SUSAN: Anyway, perhaps in the spring, it would be really nice to meet . . .

BROCK: Please don't insult my intelligence. I know you better than you think. I recognize the signs. When you talk longingly about the war . . . some deception usually follows.

(BROCK *kisses* SUSAN.)

Goodbye.

(BROCK *goes out.* SUSAN *left standing for a few moments. Then she picks up the plate and goes quickly to the kitchen.* ALICE *comes out of the bathroom at once in a dressing-gown. She has a notebook in her hand which she tosses the length of the room, so it lands on a chair. She settles on her back in the camp bed.* SUSAN *reappears at the door.*)

SUSAN: Did you hear that?

ALICE: Certainly. I was writing it down.

(SUSAN *looks across at her, but* ALICE *is putting pennies on her eyes.*)

My death-mask.

SUSAN: Don't.

ALICE: I dream better.

(*Pause.*)

SUSAN: Do you know what you're doing tomorrow?

ALICE: Not really. There's a new jazz band at the One-O-One. And Ken wants to take me to Eel Pie Island in his horrid little car. I say I'll go if I get to meet Alistair. I really do want to meet Alistair. Everyone says he's got hair on his shoulder-blades and apparently he can crack walnuts in his armpits.

SUSAN: Oh well, he'll never be short of friends.

ALICE: Quite.

(SUSAN *turns out one light. Dim light only. She looks at the parcel.*)

SUSAN: What should I be doing with this?

ALICE: If we can't eat it, let's throw it away.

(SUSAN *turns out the other light. Darkness. The sound of* SUSAN *getting into bed.*)

Your friend Brock says we're all going to be rich.

SUSAN: Oh really?

(*Pause.*)

ALICE: Peace and plenty.

SCENE 5

Temple. May 1951.

   Music, a cello leading. The Embankment, beside a lamp, overlooking the river.

   Night. SUSAN *stands, thickly wrapped. For the first time, she is expensively dressed. She is eating hot chestnuts.* MICK *appears at the back. He is from the East End. He looks twenty, smart and personable. He speaks before she knows he's there.*

MICK: Five hundred cheese-graters.

SUSAN: Oh no.

MICK: I got five hundred cheese-graters parked round the side.

Are you interested?

SUSAN: I'm afraid you're too late. We took a consignment weeks
ago.

(SUSAN *laughs*. MICK *moves down beside her*.)

MICK: Where we looking?

SUSAN: Across the river. Over there.

MICK: Where?

SUSAN: South Bank. That's where the fireworks are going to be.
And there's my barrage balloon.

MICK: Oh yeah. What does it say?

SUSAN: Don't say that, that's the worst thing you can say.

MICK: It's dark.

SUSAN: It says Bovril.

MICK: Oh Bovril.

SUSAN: Yes. It's meant to blaze out over London.

MICK: Surprised it hasn't got your name on.

SUSAN: What do you mean?

MICK: Everywhere I go.

(*Pause. They look at each other.* SUSAN *smiles and removes a napkin
from her coat pocket, and unfolds its bundle.*)

SUSAN: I managed to steal some supper from the Festival Hall.
There's a reception for its opening night. They're using
your cutlery, I'm happy to say.

MICK: I wish I could see it.

SUSAN: Yes, yes, I wish you could too. (*She smiles.*) I've actually
decided to leave the Festival now. Having worked so hard
to get the wretched thing on. I'm thinking of going into
advertising.

MICK: Ah very good.

SUSAN: I met some people on the Bovril side. It's . . . well I
doubt if it'll stretch me, but it would be a way of having
some fun. (*Pause.*) Would you like a canapé?

MICK: How's Alice?

SUSAN: She's very well.

MICK: Haven't seen her lately.

SUSAN: No.

MICK: She went mainstream you see. I stayed revivalist.

Different religion. For me it all stops in 1919.

(*He takes a canapé.*)

So how can I help?

SUSAN: I'm looking for a father. I want to have a child.

(*Pause.*)

Look, it really is much easier than it sounds. I mean, marriage is not involved. Or even looking after it. You don't even have to see the pregnancy through. I mean, conception will be the end of the job.

(MICK *smiles.*)

MICK: Ah.

SUSAN: You don't want to?

MICK: No, no, I'm delighted, I'm lucky to be asked.

SUSAN: Not at all.

MICK: But it's just . . . your own people. I mean friends, you must have friends.

SUSAN: It's . . .

MICK: I mean . . .

SUSAN: Sorry.

MICK: No, go on, say.

SUSAN: The men I know at work, at the Festival, or even friends I've known for years, they just aren't the kind of people I would want to marry.

MICK: Ah.

SUSAN: I'm afraid I'm rather strongminded, as you know, and so with them I usually feel I'm holding myself in for fear of literally blowing them out the room. They are kind, they are able, but I don't see . . . why I should have to compromise, why I should have to make some sad and decorous marriage just to have a child. I don't see why any woman should have to do that.

MICK: But you don't have to marry . . .

SUSAN: Ah well . . .

MICK: Just go off with them.

SUSAN: But that's really the problem. These same men, these kind and likeable men, they do have another side to their nature and that is they are very limited in their ideas, they are

frightened of the unknown, they want a quiet life
where sex is either sport or duty but absolutely nothing in
between, and they simply would not agree to sleep with me
if they knew it was a child I was after.

MICK: But you wouldn't have to tell them.

SUSAN: I did think that. But then I thought it would be
dishonest. And so I had the idea of asking a person whom I
barely knew.

(*Pause.*)

MICK: What about the kid?

SUSAN: What?

MICK: Doesn't sound a very good deal. Never to see his dad . . .

SUSAN: It's not . . .

MICK: I take it that is what you mean.

SUSAN: I think it's what I mean.

MICK: Well?

SUSAN: The child will manage.

MICK: How do you know?

SUSAN: Being a bastard won't always be so bad.

MICK: I wouldn't bet on it.

SUSAN: England can't be like this for ever.

(MICK *looks at her.*)

MICK: I would like to know . . .

SUSAN: Yes?

MICK: Why you chose me. I mean, how often have you met me?

SUSAN: Yes, but that's the whole point . . .

MICK: With Alice a few times . . .

SUSAN: And you sold me some spoons.

MICK: They were good spoons.

SUSAN: I'm not denying it.

(MICK *smiles.*)

MICK: And Alice says what? That I'm clean and obedient and
don't have any cretins in the family?

SUSAN: It's not as calculated as that.

MICK: Not calculated? Several hundred of us, was there, all got
notes . . .

SUSAN: No.

MICK: . . . saying come and watch the Festival fireworks, tell
   no one, bring no friends. All the secrecy, I thought you
   must at least be after nylons . . .

SUSAN: I'll buy nylons. If that's what you want.

   (*They stare at each other.*)

MICK: So why me?

SUSAN: I like you.

MICK: And?

SUSAN: 'I love you'?

   (*Pause.*)

   I chose you because . . . I don't see you very much. I barely
   ever see you. We live at opposite ends of town. Different
   worlds.

MICK: Different class.

SUSAN: That comes into it.

   (*There is a pause.* MICK *looks at her. Then moves away. Turns back.
   Smiles.*)

MICK: Oh dear.

SUSAN: Then laugh.

   (*Pause.*)

   I never met the man I wanted to marry.

   (*They smile.*)

MICK: It can't be what you want. Not deep down.

SUSAN: No.

MICK: I didn't think so.

SUSAN: Deep down I'd do the whole damn thing by myself. But
   there we are. You're second-best.

   (*They smile again.*)

MICK: Five hundred cheese-graters.

SUSAN: How much?

MICK: Something over the odds. A bit over the odds. Not much.

SUSAN: Done.

   (*Pause.*)

   Don't worry. The Festival will pay.

   (SUSAN *moves across to* MICK. *They kiss. They look at each other. He
   smiles. Then they turn and look at the night. He is barely audible.*)

MICK: Fireworks. If you . . .

SUSAN: What?

MICK: Stay for the fireworks.

SUSAN: If you like.

(*Pause.*)

MICK: Great sky.

SUSAN: Yes.

MICK: The light. Those dots.

SUSAN: A mackerel sky.

MICK: What?

SUSAN: That's what they call it. A mackerel sky.

SCENE 6

Pimlico. December 1952.

From the dark the sound of Charlie Parker and his saxophone.

Night. The bed-sitting room transformed. The beds have gone and the room is much more comforting. Three people. SUSAN *is working at her desk which is covered with papers and drawings.* ALICE *is standing over a table which has been cleared so that she may paint the naked body of* LOUISE *who lies stretched across its top. She is in her late teens, from Liverpool.* ALICE *is a good way on with the job. The record ends.*

SUSAN: This is hell.

ALICE: No doubt.

SUSAN: I am living in hell.

(SUSAN *sits back and stares at her desk.* ALICE *goes to the record player.*)

ALICE: Shall we hear it again?

SUSAN: You're only allowed it once. Hear it too much and you get out of hand.

ALICE: It's true. (*She turns it off and returns to painting.*) I'd give that up if I were you. We have to go pretty soon.

SUSAN: Why do I lie?

ALICE: We have to get there by midnight.

SUSAN: What do I do it for?

ALICE: It's your profession.

SUSAN: That's what's wrong. In France . . .

ALICE: Ah France.

SUSAN: I told such glittering lies. But where's the fun in lying for a living?

ALICE: What's today's?

SUSAN: Some leaking footwear. Some rotten shoe I have to advertise. What is the point? Why do I exist?

ALICE: Sold out.

SUSAN: Sold out. Is that the phrase?

(*Pause.* ALICE *paints.* SUSAN *stares.*)

ALICE: Turn over, let me do the other side.

(LOUISE *moves on to her stomach.*)

SUSAN: To produce what my masters call good copy, it is simply a question of pitching my intelligence low enough. Shutting my eyes and imagining what it's like to be very, very stupid. This is all the future holds for any of us. We will spend the next twenty years of our lives pretending to be thick. 'I'm sorry, Miss Traherne, we'd like to employ you, but unfortunately you are not stupid enough.'

(SUSAN *tears up the work she is doing and sits back glaring.* ALICE *explains to* LOUISE.)

ALICE: You're all trunk up to here, OK?

LOUISE: Yeah, right.

ALICE: The trunk is all one, so you just have to keep your legs together. Then you break into leaf, just above the bust.

LOUISE: Do I get conkers?

ALICE: No. If you were a chestnut, you'd get conkers. But you're an oak.

LOUISE: What does an oak have?

ALICE: An oak has acorns.

LOUISE: Acorns?

ALICE: But you won't need them, I promise you. We scorn gimmicks. We will win as we are.

SUSAN: (*To herself*) The last night of the year . . .

ALICE: And I will sell a great many paintings.

(*Pause.* ALICE *paints.*)

Louise is staying with Emma and Willy . . .

SUSAN: Oh yes?

LOUISE: I met them in the street, I'd just left home, come down the A6.

SUSAN: Good for you.

LOUISE: I couldn't believe my luck.

ALICE: Willy's going as a kipper, I do know that. And Emma's a prostitute though how we're meant to know it's fancy dress I really can't think.

LOUISE: I've gathered that.

ALICE: Otherwise I expect the usual historical riff-raff. Henry VIII, that sort of thing. We ought to walk it with a naked oak.

LOUISE: Will that friend of yours be there?

(*A moment.* SUSAN *looks across at* ALICE *and* LOUISE.)

ALICE: No. He'll be tucked up with his syphilitic wife.

LOUISE: Why doesn't he . . . ?

SUSAN: Shut up, Louise.

ALICE: It's all right. Ask what you want.

(*Pause.*)

LOUISE: How do you know she's syphilitic?

ALICE: How do you think? She passed it down the line.

LOUISE: Oh God.

ALICE: Or somebody passed it and I've decided to blame her. It seems right somehow. She's a very plausible incubator for a social disease. Back over.

(LOUISE *turns again.*)

LOUISE: Why doesn't he leave?

ALICE: Who?

LOUISE: Your friend.

ALICE: Ah well, if they ever did leave their wives, perhaps the whole sport would die. For all of us.

SUSAN: Roll on 1953.

(ALICE *smiles and resumes painting.*)

ALICE: Actually the clinic say it's non-specific urethritis, which I find rather insulting. I did at least expect the doctor to come out and apologize and say, I'm sorry not to be more specific about your urethritis, but no, they just leave you in the air.

(*As she is talking* MICK *has appeared at the door.*)

MICK: I wonder, does anyone mind if I come in?

ALICE: Mick?

(MICK *moves into the room.*)

MICK: Would you mind if I . . . ?

SUSAN: How did you get this address?

ALICE: Do you two know each other?

MICK: Happy New Year.

(*Pause.*)

ALICE: Mick, may I introduce you to Louise.

LOUISE: Hello, Mick.

MICK: Hello, Louise.

ALICE: Louise is going to the Arts Ball, I'm painting her . . .

MICK: Ah.

ALICE: She's going as a tree.

SUSAN: Mick, I really don't want to talk to you.

ALICE: What's wrong?

MICK: Is she really going to walk down the street . . .

SUSAN: I thought we'd agreed. You promised me, Mick. You made a promise. Never to meet again.

(*A pause.* MICK *looks down.*)

MICK: I just thought . . . well it's New Year's Eve and well . . . one or two weeks have gone by . . .

SUSAN: Have you been watching the house? Is that how you found me? Have you been following me home? (*She stares across at him.*)

Look, Mick, I suggest that you leave while you still have the chance.

(LOUISE *has swung down from the table.*)

LOUISE: Does anyone mind if I put my clothes on?

(*In the silence she picks up her clothes and goes into the kitchen.*
ALICE *speaks quietly.*)

ALICE: She's not finished. She'll look good when it's done.

(*Pause.*)

SUSAN: I asked Mick to father a child, that's what we're talking about.

MICK: Oh Christ.

SUSAN: Well we have tried over eighteen months, that's right? And we have failed.

MICK: Right.

SUSAN: Which leaves us both feeling pretty stupid, pretty wretched I would guess, speaking for myself. And there is a point of decency at which the experiment should stop.

MICK: Susan . . .

SUSAN: We have nothing in common, never did, that was part of the idea . . .

MICK: It just feels bad . . .

SUSAN: The idea was fun, it was simple, it depended on two adults behaving like adults . . .

MICK: It feels very bad to be used.

SUSAN: I would have stopped it months ago, I would have stopped it in the second month . . .

MICK: You come out feeling dirty.

SUSAN: And how do I feel? What am I meant to feel? Crawling about in your tiny bedroom, paper-thin walls, your mother sitting downstairs . . .

MICK: Don't bring my mum into this.

SUSAN: Scrabbling about on bombsites, you think I enjoy all that?

MICK: Yeah. Very much. I think you do.

(*Pause.* ALICE *looks away.* SUSAN *moves quietly away as if to give it up.* MICK *calms down.*)

I just think . . .

SUSAN: I know what you think. You think I enjoy slumming around. Then why have I not looked for another father? Because the whole exploit has broken my heart.

(*Pause.*)

MICK: You think it's my fault.

SUSAN: Oh Lord, is that all you're worried about?

MICK: You think it's something to do with me?

SUSAN: That was part of it, never to have to drag through this kind of idiot argument . . .

MICK: Well it is quite important.

SUSAN: You don't understand. You don't understand the figures in my mind.

(*Pause.*)

Mick, there is gentlemen's footwear. It must be celebrated. I have to find words to convey the sensation of walking round London on two pieces of reconstituted cardboard stuck together with horseglue. And I have to find them tonight. (SUSAN *goes to her desk, takes out fresh paper. Starts work.* LOUISE *comes from the kitchen, plainly dressed.*)

LOUISE: I'll tell the others. You may be late.

(ALICE *stoops down and picks up a couple of papiermâché green branches.*)

ALICE: There are some branches. You have to tie them round your wrists.

LOUISE: Thanks all the same. I'll just go as myself.

(LOUISE *goes out. There is a silence, as* SUSAN *works at her desk.* ALICE *sits with her hand over her eyes.* MICK *sits miserably staring. This goes on for some time until finally* SUSAN *speaks very quietly, without looking up from her desk.*)

SUSAN: Mick, will you go now please?

MICK: You people are cruel.

SUSAN: Please.

MICK: You are cruel and dangerous.

SUSAN: Mick.

MICK: You fuck people up. This little tart and her string of married men, all fucked up, all fucking ruined by this tart. And you . . . and you . . .

(MICK *turns to* SUSAN. SUSAN *gets up and walks quietly from the room. A pause.* ALICE *is looking at him.*)

She is actually mad.

(SUSAN *reappears with her revolver. She fires it just over* MICK'*s head. It is deafeningly loud. He falls to the ground. She fires three more times.*)

MICK: Jesus Christ.

SCENE 7

Knightsbridge. October 1956.
   From the dark, music, emphatic, triumphant.
   The room we saw in Scene 1. But now decorated with heavy velvet
curtains, china objects and soft furniture. A diplomatic home. Both men in
dinner-jackets: BROCK *smokes a cigar and drinks brandy. Opposite him is*
an almost permanently smiling Burmese, M. AUNG, *short, dogmatic. The*
music stops.

AUNG: Two great nations, sir. The Americans and the English.
   Like the Romans and the Greeks. Americans are the
   Romans—power, armies, strength. The English are the
   Greeks—ideas, civilization, intellect. Between them they
   shall rule the world.
   (DARWIN *appears putting his head round the door. He is also in a*
   dinner-jacket. He appears exhausted.)
DARWIN: Good Lord, I hope you haven't hung on for me.
BROCK: Leonard, come in, how kind of you to come.
DARWIN: Not at all.
   (BROCK *ushers him in.* AUNG *stands.*)
BROCK: Our little gathering. We'd scarcely dared hope . . .
DARWIN: There seemed nothing left to do.
BROCK: Leonard, you know M. Aung, of course?
AUNG: Mr Darwin.
DARWIN: Rangoon.
BROCK: Now First Secretary, Burmese Embassy.
AUNG: An honour. A privilege. A moment in my career. I shake
   your hand. (*He does so.*)
DARWIN: Good, good. Well . . .
BROCK: Let me get you a drink.
DARWIN: That would be very kind.
BROCK: I'll just tell my wife you're here.
   (BROCK *goes out.* AUNG *smiles at* DARWIN.)

171

AUNG: Affairs of state?

DARWIN: Yes, if you . . .

AUNG: Say no more. We have eaten. We did not wait. In Burma
we say if you cannot be on time, do not come at all.

DARWIN: Really?

AUNG: But of course the English it is different. At your
command the lion makes its bed with the lamb.

DARWIN: Hardly.

AUNG: Don't worry. All will be well. Ah Darwin of Djakarta, to
have met the man, to have been alone with him. I shall
dine in on this for many years.

DARWIN: Dine out on this.

AUNG: Ah the English language, she is a demanding mistress,
yes?

DARWIN: If you like.

AUNG: And no one controls her so well as you sir. You beat her
and the bitch obeys. (*He laughs.*) The language of the world.
Good, good. I have learnt the phrase from you. Out of your
mouth. Good, good. I am behind you sir.

(SUSAN *appears in a superbly cut evening dress. She is dangerously
cheerful.* BROCK *follows her.*)

SUSAN: Leonard, how good of you to make an appearance.

DARWIN: I'm only sorry I've been delayed.

(SUSAN *and* DARWIN *kiss.*)

SUSAN: Brock says you're all ragged with fatigue. I hear you've
been having the most frightful week . . .

DARWIN: It has been, yes.

SUSAN: Well, don't worry. Here at least you can relax. You've
met Mr Aung?

DARWIN: Indeed.

SUSAN: You can forget everything. The words 'Suez Canal' will
not be spoken.

DARWIN: That will be an enormous relief.

SUSAN: They are banned, you will not hear them.

DARWIN: Thank you, my dear.

SUSAN: Nasser, nobody will mention his name.

DARWIN: Quite.

SUSAN: Nobody will say blunder or folly or fiasco. Nobody will
say 'international laughing stock'. You are among friends,
Leonard. I will rustle up some food.
(*She smiles at* AUNG.)
Mr Aung, I think the gentlemen may wish to talk.
AUNG: Of course, in such company I am privileged to change
sex.
(AUNG *gets up to follow* SUSAN *out*.)
SUSAN: Nobody will say 'death-rattle of the ruling class'. We
have stuck our lips together with marron glacé. I hope you
understand.
(SUSAN *and* AUNG *go out. Pause.*)
BROCK: Sorry, I . . .
DARWIN: It's all right.
BROCK: I did ask her to calm down.
DARWIN: I'm getting used to it.
BROCK: She's been giving me hell. She knows how closely you've
been involved . . .
DARWIN: Do you think we could leave the subject, Brock?
(*Pause.*)
I'm eager for the drink.
BROCK: Of course.
DARWIN: At least she got rid of that appalling wog. I mean, in
honesty, Raymond, what are you trying to do to me?
BROCK: I'm sorry, sir.
DARWIN: This week of all weeks. He had his tongue stuck so far
up my fundament all you could see of him were the soles of
his feet.
(BROCK *takes over a tray of drinks*.)
Mental illness, is it? Your wife?
BROCK: No, no she just . . . feels very strongly. Well, you
know . . .
DARWIN: But there has been mental illness?
BROCK: In the past.
DARWIN: Yes?
BROCK: Before we were married. Some years ago. She'd been
living very foolishly, a loose set in Pimlico. And a series of

jobs, pushing herself too hard. Not eating. We got
engaged when she was still quite ill, and I have tried to
help her back up.

DARWIN: That's very good.

BROCK: Well . . .

DARWIN: Second marriage, of course. Often stabilizes.

BROCK: What?

DARWIN: The chap in Brussels.

(*Pause.*)

The stiff.

BROCK: Ah yes.

DARWIN: You don't have to be ashamed . . .

BROCK: No, I'm not, it's . . .

DARWIN: In the diplomatic service it isn't as if a mad wife is any
kind of professional disadvantage. On the contrary, it
almost guarantees promotion.

BROCK: Well . . .

DARWIN: Some of the senior men, their wives are absolutely
barking. I take the word 'gouache' to be the giveaway.
When they start drifting out of rooms saying, 'I think I'll
just go and do my gouaches dear,' then you know you've
lost them for good and all.

BROCK: But Susan isn't mad.

DARWIN: No, no.

(*Pause.*)

Is there a Madame Aung?

BROCK: In the other room.

DARWIN: I knew there had to be. Somehow. And no doubt
culturally inclined. Traditional dance, she'll tell us about,
in the highlands of Burma. Or the plot of *Lohengrin*.

BROCK: Leonard . . .

DARWIN: I'm sorry. I think I've had it, Brock. One more Aung
and I throw in the can.

(*Pause.*)

Do you mind if I have a cherry?

BROCK: What?

DARWIN: The maraschinos. I'm so hungry. It's all those bloody drugs we have to take.

BROCK: Let me . . .

DARWIN: Stay.

(*Pause.*)

We have been betrayed.

(DARWIN *reaches into the cocktail cherries with his fingers, but then just rolls them slowly in his palm.*)

We claim to be intervening as a neutral party in a dispute between Israel and Egypt. Last Monday the Israelis launched their attack. On Tuesday we issued our ultimatum saying both sides must withdraw to either side of the canal. But, Raymond, the Israelis, the aggressors, they were nowhere near the canal. They'd have had to advance a hundred miles to make the retreat.

BROCK: Who told you that?

DARWIN: Last week the Foreign Secretary went abroad. I was not briefed. We believe he met with the French and the Israelis, urged the Israelis to attack. I believe our ultimatum was written in France last week, hence the mistake in the wording. The Israelis had reckoned to reach the canal, but met with unexpectedly heavy resistance. I think the entire war is a fraud cooked up by the British as an excuse for seizing the canal. And we, we who have to execute this policy, even we were not told.

(*Pause.*)

BROCK: Well . . . what difference does it make?

DARWIN: My dear boy.

BROCK: I mean it.

DARWIN: Raymond.

BROCK: It makes no difference.

DARWIN: I was lied to.

BROCK: Yes, but you were against it from the start.

DARWIN: I . . .

BROCK: Oh come on, we all were. The Foreign Office hated the operation from the very first mention, so what difference does it make now?

DARWIN: All the difference in the world.

BROCK: None at all.

DARWIN: The government lied to me.

BROCK: If the policy was wrong, if it was wrong to begin
with . . .

DARWIN: They are not in good faith.

BROCK: I see, I see, so what you're saying is, the British may do
anything, doesn't matter how murderous, doesn't matter
how silly, just so long as we do it in good faith.

DARWIN: Yes. I would have defended it, I wouldn't have minded
how damn stupid it was. I would have defended it had it
been honestly done. But this time we are cowboys and
when the English are the cowboys, then in truth I fear for
the future of the globe.

(*A pause.* DARWIN *walks to the curtained window and stares out.*
BROCK *left sitting doesn't turn as he speaks.*)

BROCK: Eden is weak. For years he has been weak. For years people
have taunted him, why aren't you strong? Like Churchill? He
goes round, he begins to think I must find somebody to be
strong on. He finds Nasser. Now he'll show them. He does it to
impress. He does it badly. No one is impressed.

(DARWIN *turns to look at* BROCK.)

Mostly what we do is what we think people expect of us.
Mostly it's wrong.

(*Pause.*)

Are you going to resign?

(*The sound of laughter as* SUSAN, MME AUNG, M. AUNG *and*
ALICE *stream into the room.* MME AUNG *is small, tidy and bright.*
ALICE *is spectacularly dressed.*)

SUSAN: Mme Aung has been enthralling us with the story of the
new Bergman film at the Everyman.

DARWIN: Ah.

BROCK: Ah yes.

SUSAN: Apparently it's about depression, isn't that so, Mme
Aung?

MME AUNG: I do feel the Norwegians are very good at that sort of
thing.

SUSAN: Is anything wrong?

(SUSAN *stands and looks at* BROCK *and* DARWIN.)

Please do sit down everyone. I'm sorry, I think we may have interrupted the men.

BROCK: It's all right.

SUSAN: They were probably drafting a telegram . . .

BROCK: We weren't . . .

SUSAN: That's what they do before they drop a bomb. They send their targets notice in a telegram. Bombs tonight, evacuate the area. Now what does that indicate to you, M. Aung?

BROCK: Susan, please.

SUSAN: I'll tell you what it indicates to me. Bad conscience. They don't even have the guts to make a war any more.

(*Pause.*)

DARWIN: Perhaps Mme Aung will tell us the story of the film. This is something I'd be very keen to hear.

MME AUNG: I feel the ladies have already . . .

ALICE: We don't mind.

SUSAN: It's all right. Go ahead. We like the bit in the mental ward.

MME AUNG: Ah yes.

SUSAN: Raymond will like it. You got me at the Maudsley, didn't you dear?

BROCK: Yes, yes.

SUSAN: That's where he proposed to me. A moment of weakness. Of mine, I mean.

BROCK: Please, darling . . .

SUSAN: I married him because he reminded me of my father.

MME AUNG: Really?

SUSAN: At that point, of course, I didn't realize just what a shit my father was.

(*Pause.*)

ALICE: I'm sorry. She has a sort of psychiatric cabaret.

(SUSAN *laughs.*)

SUSAN: That's very good. And there's something about Suez which . . .

BROCK: Will you please be quiet?

(*Pause.*)

The story of the film.

(MME AUNG *is embarrassed. It takes her considerable effort to start.*)

MME AUNG: There's a woman . . . who despises her husband . . .
(*Pause.*)

SUSAN: Is it getting a little bit chilly in here? October nights.
Those poor parachutists. I do know how they feel. Even
now. Cities. Fields. Trees. Farms. Dark spaces. Lights. The
parachute opens. We descend.
(*Pause.*)
Of course, we were comparatively welcome, not always
ecstatic, not the Gaullists, of course, but by and large we
did make it our business to land in countries where we were
wanted. Certainly the men were. I mean, some of the
relationships, I can't tell you. I remember a colleague
telling me of the heat, of the smell of a particular young
girl, the hot wet smell, he said. Nothing since. Nothing
since then. I can't see the Egyptian girls somehow . . . no.
Not in Egypt now. I mean, there were broken hearts when
we left. I mean, there are girls today who mourn
Englishmen who died in Dachau, died naked in Dachau,
men with whom they had spent a single night. Well.
(*Pause. The tears are pouring down* SUSAN*'s face, she can barely
speak.*)
But then . . . even for myself I do like to make a point of
sleeping with men I don't know. I do find once you get to
know them you usually don't want to sleep with them any
more . . .
(BROCK *gets up and shouts at the top of his voice across the room.*)

BROCK: Please can you stop, can you stop fucking talking for five
fucking minutes on end?

SUSAN: I would stop, I would stop, I would stop fucking talking
if I ever heard anyone else say anything worth fucking
stopping talking for.
(*Pause. Then* DARWIN *moves.*)

DARWIN: I'm sorry. I apologize. I really must go.
(*He crosses the room.*)

M. Aung. Farewell.

AUNG: We are behind you, sir. There is wisdom in your
    expedition.

DARWIN: Thank you.

AUNG: May I say, sir, these gyps need whipping and you are the
    man to do it?

DARWIN: Thank you very much. Mme Aung.

MME AUNG: We never really met.

DARWIN: No. No. We never met, that is true. But perhaps before
    I go, I may nevertheless set you right on a point of fact.
    Ingmar Bergman is not a bloody Norwegian, he is a bloody
    Swede. (*He nods slightly.*) Good night, everyone.

    (DARWIN *goes out.* BROCK *gets up and goes to the door, then turns.*)

BROCK: He's going to resign.

    (*Pause.*)

SUSAN: Isn't this an exciting week? Don't you think? Isn't this
    thrilling? Don't you think? Everything is up for grabs. At last.
    We will see some changes. Thank the Lord. Now, there was
    dinner. I made some more dinner for Leonard. A little ham.
    And chicken. And some pickles and tomato. And lettuce. And
    there are a couple of pheasants in the fridge. And I can get
    twelve bottles of claret from the cellar. Why not?
    There is plenty.
    Shall we eat again?

INTERVAL

SCENE 8

Knightsbridge. July 1961.
    From the dark the voice of a PRIEST.

PRIEST: Man that is born of woman hath but a short time to live
    and is full of misery. He cometh up and is cut down like a
    flower. He fleeth and never continueth in one stay. In the

midst of life we are in death. Of whom may we seek for
succour but of thee, O Lord, who for our sins art justly
displeased?

(*The room is dark. All the chairs, all the furniture, all the mirrors
are covered in white dust-sheets. There is a strong flood of light from
the hall which silhouettes the group of three as they enter, all dressed
in black. First* BROCK, *then* DORCAS, *a tall heavily-built,
17-year-old blonde and then* ALICE *who, like the others, does not
remove her coat.* ALICE'*s manner has darkened and sharpened
somewhat.* BROCK *goes to take the sheets off two chairs.*)

BROCK: I must say, I'd forgotten just how grim it can be.

ALICE: All that mumbling.

BROCK: I know. And those bloody hymns. They really do you no
good at all. (*He wraps a sheet over his arm.*) Would you like to
sit down in here? I'm afraid the whole house is horribly
unused.

(*The women sit.* BROCK *holds his hand out to* DORCAS.)
You and I haven't had a proper chance to meet.

ALICE: I hope you didn't mind . . .

BROCK: Not at all.

ALICE: . . . my bringing Dorcas along.

BROCK: She swelled the numbers.

DORCAS: I had the afternoon off school.

BROCK: I'm not sure I'd have chosen a funeral . . .

DORCAS: It was fine.

BROCK: Oh good.

DORCAS: Alice told me that you were very good friends . . .

BROCK: Well, we are.

DORCAS: . . . who she hadn't seen for a very long time and she
was sure you wouldn't mind me . . . you know . . .

BROCK: Gatecrashing?

DORCAS: Yes.

BROCK: At the grave.

DORCAS: It sounds awful.

BROCK: You were welcome as far as I was concerned.

DORCAS: The only thing was . . . I never heard his name.

BROCK: His name was Darwin.

DORCAS: Ah.

(SUSAN *stands unremarked in the doorway. She has taken her coat off and is plainly dressed in black, with some books under her arm. Her manner is quieter than before, and yet more elegant.*)

SUSAN: Please, nobody get up for me.

(SUSAN *moves down to the front where there are two cases filled with books on the floor.*)

BROCK: Ah Susan . . .

SUSAN: I was just looking out some more books to take back.

BROCK: Are you all right?

SUSAN: Yes, fine.

ALICE: Susan, this is Dorcas I told you about.

SUSAN: How do you do?

DORCAS: How do you do?

(SUSAN *tucks the books away.*)

ALICE: I teach Dorcas history.

BROCK: Good Lord, how long have you done that?

ALICE: Oh . . . I've been at it some time.

DORCAS: Alice is a very good teacher, you know.

BROCK: I'm sure.

ALICE: Thank you, Dorcas.

DORCAS: We had a poll and Alice came top.

(*They smile at each other. Unasked,* DORCAS *gives* ALICE *a cigarette.*)

ALICE: Ta.

BROCK: Where do you teach?

ALICE: It's called the Kensington Academy.

BROCK: I see.

ALICE: It's in Shepherd's Bush.

DORCAS: It's a crammer.

ALICE: For the daughters of the rich and the congenitally stupid. Dorcas to a T.

DORCAS: It's true.

ALICE: There's almost nothing that a teacher can do.

DORCAS: Alice says we're all the prisoners of our genes.

ALICE: When you actually try to engage their attention, you know that all they can really hear inside their heads is the

181

great thump-thump of their ancestors fucking too
freely among themselves.

DORCAS: Nothing wrong with that.

ALICE: No?

DORCAS: Stupid people are happier.

ALICE: Is that what you think?

(*They smile again.* BROCK *watches.*)

BROCK: Well . . .

SUSAN: Raymond, could you manage to make us some tea?

BROCK: Certainly, if there's time . . .

SUSAN: I'm sure everyone's in need of it.

(BROCK *smiles and goes out.*)

Alice rang me this morning. She said she was very keen we
should meet.

ALICE: I didn't realize you were going back so soon.

SUSAN: It's a problem, I'm afraid. My husband is a diplomat.
We're posted in Iran. I haven't been to London for over
three years. Then when I heard of Leonard's death I
felt . . . I just felt very strongly I wanted to attend.

DORCAS: Alice was saying he'd lost a lot of his friends.

(SUSAN *looks across at* ALICE.)

SUSAN: Yes, that's true.

DORCAS: I didn't understand what . . .

SUSAN: He spoke his mind over Suez. In public. He didn't hide
his disgust. A lot of people never forgave him for that.

DORCAS: Oh I see.

(*Pause.*)

DORCAS: What's . . .

ALICE: It's a historical incident four years ago, caused a minor
kind of stir at the time. It's also the name of a waterway in
Egypt. Egypt is the big brown country up the top
right-hand corner of Africa. Africa is a continent . . .

DORCAS: Yes, thank you.

ALICE: And that's why nobody was there today.

(ALICE *looks up at* SUSAN *but she has turned away.*)

I got that panic, you know, you get at funerals. I was
thinking, I really don't want to think about death . . .

SUSAN: Yes.

ALICE: Anything, count the bricks, count the trees, but don't think about death . . . (*She smiles.*) So I tried to imagine Leonard was still alive, I mean locked in his coffin but still alive. And I was laughing at how he would have dealt with the situation, I mean just exactly what the protocol would be.

SUSAN: He would know it.

ALICE: Of course. Official procedure in the case of being buried alive. How many times one may tap on the lid. How to rise from the grave without drawing unnecessary attention to yourself.

SUSAN: Poor Leonard.

ALICE: I know. But he did make me laugh.

(SUSAN *looks at her catching the old phrase. Then turns at once to* DORCAS.)

SUSAN: Alice said I might help you in some way.

DORCAS: Well, yes.

SUSAN: Of course. If there's anything at all. (*She smiles.*)

DORCAS: Did she tell you what the problem was?

ALICE: There isn't any problem. You need money, that's all.

DORCAS: Alice said you'd once been a great friend of hers, part of her sort of crowd . . .

SUSAN: Are they still going then?

ALICE: They certainly are.

DORCAS: And that you might be sympathetic as you'd . . . well . . . as you'd known some troubles yourself . . .

ALICE: Dorcas needs cash from an impeccable source.

(*Pause.*)

SUSAN: I see.

DORCAS: I'd pay it back.

SUSAN: Well, I'm sure.

DORCAS: I mean it's only two hundred pounds. In theory I could still get it for myself, perhaps I'll have to, but Alice felt . . .

ALICE: Never mind.

DORCAS: No, I think I should, I mean, I think I should say Alice did feel as she'd introduced me to this man . . .

(*Pause.* ALICE *looks away.*)

Just because he was one of her friends . . . which I just think is silly, I mean, for God's sake, I'm old enough to live my own life . . .

SUSAN: Yes.

DORCAS: I mean, I am seventeen. And I knew what I was doing. So why the hell should Alice feel responsible?

SUSAN: I don't know.

DORCAS: Anyway the man was a doctor, one of Alice's famous bent doctors, you know, I just wanted to get hold of some drugs, but he wouldn't hand over unless I agreed to fool around, so I just . . . I didn't think anything of it . . .

SUSAN: No.

DORCAS: It just seemed like part of the price. At the time. Of course I never guessed it would be three months later and, wham, the knitting needles.

SUSAN: Yes.

(*Pause.*)

DORCAS: I mean, to be honest I could still go to Daddy and tell him. Just absolutely outright tell him. Just say, Daddy I'm sorry but . . .

ALICE: Wham the knitting needles.

DORCAS: Yes.

(SUSAN *looks across at* ALICE. *The two women stare steadily at each other as* DORCAS *talks.*)

But of course one would need a great deal of guts.

(*Pause.*)

DORCAS: I mean I can't tell you how awful I feel. I mean, coming straight from a funeral . . .

(SUSAN *suddenly gets up and walks to the door, speaking very quietly.*)

SUSAN: Well, I'm sure it needn't delay us for too long . . .

DORCAS: Do you mean . . .

SUSAN: Kill a child. That's easy. No problem at all.

(SUSAN *opens the door. She has heard* BROCK *with the tea-tray outside.*)

Ah Raymond, the tea.

BROCK: I have to tell you the car has arrived.

SUSAN: Oh good.

BROCK: The driver is saying we must get away at once.

(SUSAN *has gone out into the hall.* BROCK *sets the tray down near* DORCAS *and* ALICE, *and begins to pour.*)

BROCK: It must be two years since I made my own tea. Persian labour is disgustingly cheap.

DORCAS: I thought you said they . . .

ALICE: It's another name for Iran.

DORCAS: Oh I see.

(SUSAN *has reappeared with her handbag and now goes to the writing desk. She folds the sheet back and lowers the lid.*)

BROCK: Susan I do hope you're preparing to go.

SUSAN: I will do, I just need a minute or two . . .

BROCK: I don't think we have time to do anything but . . .

(SUSAN *walks over to him.*)

SUSAN: I do need some tea. Just to wash down my pill.

(*A pause.* BROCK *smiles.*)

BROCK: Yes, of course.

(SUSAN *takes the cup from his hand. Then goes back to the desk where she gets out a cheque book and begins to write.*)

ALICE: So, Raymond, you must tell us about life in Iran.

BROCK: I would say we'd been very happy out there. Wouldn't you, Susan?

SUSAN: Uh-huh.

BROCK: I think the peace has done us both a great deal of good. We were getting rather frenzied in our last few months here. (*He smiles.*)

ALICE: And the people?

BROCK: The people are fine. In so far as one's seen them, you know. It's only occasionally that you manage to get out. But the trips are startling, no doubt about that. There you are.

(BROCK *hands* ALICE *tea.*)

ALICE: Thank you.

BROCK: The sky. The desert. And of course the poverty. Living among people who have to struggle so hard. It can make you see life very differently.

SUSAN: Do I make it to cash?

ALICE: If you could.

(BROCK *hands* DORCAS *tea.*)

DORCAS: Thanks.

BROCK: I do remember Leonard, that Leonard always said, the pleasure of diplomacy is perspective, you see. Looking across distances. For instance, we see England very clearly from there. And it does look just a trifle decadent. (*He smiles again and drinks his tea.*)

SUSAN: I'm lending Dorcas some money.

BROCK: Oh really, is that wise?

ALICE: She needs an operation.

BROCK: What?

ALICE: The tendons of her hands. If she's ever to play in a concert hall again.

BROCK: Do you actually play a . . .

(SUSAN *gets up from her desk.*)

SUSAN: Raymond, could you take a look at that case? One of those locks is refusing to turn.

BROCK: Ah yes.

(BROCK *goes to shut the case.* ALICE *watches smiling as* SUSAN *walks across to* DORCAS *to hand her the cheque.*)

SUSAN: Here you are.

DORCAS: Thank you.

SUSAN: Don't thank us. We're rotten with cash.

(BROCK *closes the case.* SUSAN *gathers the cups on to the tray and places it by the door.*)

BROCK: If that's it, then I reckon we're ready to go. I'm sorry to turn you out of the house . . .

ALICE: That's all right.

BROCK: Alice, you must come and see us . . .

ALICE: I shall.

BROCK: My tour has been extended another two years. Dorcas, I'm happy to have met. I hope your studies proceed, under Alice's tutelage. In the meanwhile perhaps you might lend me a hand . . . (*He gestures at the case.*) Susan's lifeline. Her case full of books.

(DORCAS *goes to carry out the smaller case.*)

Susan, you're ready?

SUSAN: Yes, I am.

BROCK: You'll follow me down?

(SUSAN *nods but doesn't move.*)

Well . . . I shall be waiting in the car.

(BROCK *goes out with the large case.* DORCAS *follows.*)

DORCAS: Alice, we won't be long will we?

ALICE: No.

DORCAS: It's just it's biology tonight and that's my favourite.

(*Off.*) Do I put them in the boot?

BROCK: (*Off*) If you could.

(SUSAN *and* ALICE *left alone do not move. A pause.*)

SUSAN: I knew if I came over I would never return.

(*She pulls the sheet off the desk. It slinks on to the floor. Then she moves round the room, pulling away all the sheets from the furniture, letting them all fall. Then takes them from the mirrors. Then she lights the standard lamps, the table lamps. The room warms and brightens.* ALICE *sits perfectly still, her legs outstretched. Then* SUSAN *turns to look at* ALICE.)

You excite me.

(BROCK *appears at the open door.*)

BROCK: Susan. Darling. Are we ready to go?

SCENE 9

Whitehall. January 1962.

From the dark the sound of a radio interview. The INTERVIEWER *is male, serious, a little guarded.*

VOICE: You were one of the few women to be flown into France?

SUSAN: Yes.

VOICE: And one of the youngest?

SUSAN: Yes.

VOICE: Did you always have complete confidence in the
   organization that sent you?

SUSAN: Yes, of course.

VOICE: Since the war it's frequently been alleged that Special
   Operations was amateurish, its recruitment methods were
   haphazard, some of its behaviour was rather cavalier. Did
   you feel that at the time?

SUSAN: Not at all.

VOICE: The suggestion is that it was careless of human life. Did
   you feel that any of your colleagues died needlessly?

SUSAN: I can't say.

VOICE: If you were to . . .

SUSAN: Sorry, if I could . . . ?

VOICE: By all means.

SUSAN: You believed in the organization. You had to. If you
   didn't, you would die.

VOICE: But you must have had an opinion . . .

SUSAN: No. I had no opinion. I have an opinion now.

VOICE: And that is?

SUSAN: That it was one part of the war from which the British
   emerge with the greatest possible valour and distinction.
   (*A slight pause.*)

VOICE: Do you ever get together with former colleagues and talk
   about the war?

SUSAN: Never. We aren't clubbable.

(*The Foreign Office. A large room in Scott's Palazzo. A mighty painting
above a large fireplace in an otherwise barish waiting room. It shows
Britannia Colonorum Mater in pseudo-classical style. Otherwise the room
is uncheering. A functional desk, some unremarkable wooden chairs, a
green radiator. An air of functional disuse. Two people.* SUSAN *is standing
at one side smartly dressed again with coat and handbag;* BEGLEY *stands
opposite by an inner door. He is a thin young man with impeccable
manners. He is 22.*)

BEGLEY: Mrs Brock, Sir Andrew will see you now. He only has a
   few minutes, I'm afraid.

   (*At once through the inner door comes* SIR ANDREW CHARLESON *in a double-breasted blue suit. He is in his early fifties, dark-haired, thickening, almost indolent. He cuts less of a figure than* DARWIN *but he has far more edge.*)

CHARLESON: Ah Mrs Brock.

SUSAN: Sir Andrew.

CHARLESON: How do you do?

(SUSAN *and* CHARLESON *shake hands.*)

CHARLESON: We have met.

SUSAN: That's right.

CHARLESON: The Queen's Garden Party. And I've heard you on the wireless only recently. Talking about the war. How extraordinary it must have been.

(*Pause.*)

SUSAN: This must seem a very strange request.

CHARLESON: Not in the slightest. We're delighted to see you here.

(BEGLEY *takes two chairs out from the wall and places them down opposite each other.*)

Perhaps I might offer you a drink.

SUSAN: If you are having one.

CHARLESON: Unfortunately not. I'm somewhat liverish.

SUSAN: I'm sorry.

CHARLESON: No, no, it's a hazard of the job. Half the diplomats I know have bad offal, I'm afraid. (*He turns to* BEGLEY.) If you could leave us, Begley . . .

BEGLEY: Sir.

CHARLESON: Just shuffle some papers for a while.

(BEGLEY *goes through the inner door.* CHARLESON *gestures* SUSAN *to sit.*)

You mustn't be nervous, you know, Mrs Brock. I have to encounter many diplomatic wives, many even more distinguished than yourself, with very similar intent. It is much commoner than you suppose.

SUSAN: Sir Andrew, as you know I take very little part in my husband's professional life . . .

CHARLESON: Indeed.

SUSAN: Normally I spend a great deal of time on my own . . .

with one or two friends . . . of my own . . . Mostly I like
reading, I like reading alone . . . I do think to be merely
your husband's wife is demeaning for a woman of any
integrity at all . . .

(CHARLESON *smiles*.)

CHARLESON: I understand.

SUSAN: But I find for the first time in my husband's career I am
beginning to feel some need to intervene.

CHARLESON: I had a message, yes.

SUSAN: I hope you appreciate my loyalty . . .

CHARLESON: Oh yes.

SUSAN: Coming here at all. Brock is a man who has seen me
through some very difficult times . . .

CHARLESON: I am told.

SUSAN: But this is a matter on which I need to go behind his
back.

(CHARLESON *gestures reassurance*.)

My impression is that since our recall from Iran he is in
some way being penalized.

(CHARLESON *makes no reaction*.)

As I understand it, you're Head of Personnel . . .

CHARLESON: I'm the Chief Clerk, yes . . .

SUSAN: I've come to ask exactly what my husband's prospects
are.

(*Pause*.)

I do understand the foreign service now. I know that my
husband could never ask himself. Your business is
conducted in a code, which it's considered unethical to
break. Signs and indications are all you are given. Your
stock is rising, your stock is falling . . .

CHARLESON: Yes.

SUSAN: Brock has been allocated to a fairly lowly job, backing up
the EEC negotiating team . . .

CHARLESON: He's part of the push into Europe, yes.

SUSAN: The foreign posts he's since been offered have not been
glittering.

CHARLESON: We offered him Monrovia.

SUSAN: Monrovia. Yes. He took that to be an insult. Was he wrong?

(CHARLESON *smiles*.)

CHARLESON: Monrovia is not an insult.

SUSAN: But?

CHARLESON: Monrovia is more in the nature of a test. A test of nerve, it's true. If a man is stupid enough to accept Monrovia, then he probably deserves Monrovia. That is how we think.

SUSAN: But you . . .

CHARLESON: And Brock refused. (*He shrugs*.) Had we wanted to insult him there are far worse jobs. In this building too. In my view town-twinning is the *coup de grâce*. I'd far rather be a martyr to the tsetse fly than have to twin Rotherham with Bergen-op-Zoom.

SUSAN: You are evading me.

(*Pause.* CHARLESON *smiles again*.)

CHARLESON: I'm sorry. It's a habit, as you say. (*He pauses to rethink. Then with confidence*) Your husband has never been a flyer, Mrs Brock.

SUSAN: I see.

CHARLESON: Everyone is streamed, a slow stream, a fast stream . . .

SUSAN: My husband is slow?

CHARLESON: Slowish.

SUSAN: That means . . .

CHARLESON: What is he? First Secretary struggling towards Counsellor. At forty-one it's not remarkable, you know.

SUSAN: But it's got worse.

CHARLESON: You think?

SUSAN: The last six months. He's never felt excluded from his work before.

CHARLESON: Does he feel that?

SUSAN: I think you know he does.

(*Pause*.)

CHARLESON: Well, I'm sure the intention was not to punish him. We have had some trouble in placing him, it's true. The rather startling decision to desert his post . . .

SUSAN: That was not his fault.

CHARLESON: We were told. We were sympathetic. Psychiatric reasons?

SUSAN: I was daunted at the prospect of returning to Iran.

CHARLESON: Of course. Persian psychiatry. I shudder at the thought. A heavy-handed people at the best of times. We understood. Family problems. Our sympathy goes out . . .

SUSAN: But you are blocking his advance.

(CHARLESON *thinks, then changes tack again.*)

CHARLESON: I think you should understand the basis of our talk. The basis on which I agreed to talk. You asked for information. The information is this: that Brock is making haste slowly. That is all I can say.

SUSAN: I'm very keen he should not suffer on my account.

(SUSAN*'s voice is low.* CHARLESON *looks at his hands.*)

CHARLESON: Mrs Brock, believe me I recognize your tone. Women have come in here and used it before.

SUSAN: I would like to see my husband advance.

CHARLESON: I also have read the stories in your file, so nothing in your manner is likely to amaze. I do know exactly the kind of person you are. When you have chosen a particular course . . . (*He pauses.*) When there is something which you very badly want . . . (*He pauses again.*) But in this matter I must tell you, Mrs Brock, it is more than likely you have met your match.

(*The two of them stare straight at each other.*)

We are talking of achievement at the highest level. Brock cannot expect to be cosseted through. It's not enough to be clever. Everyone here is clever, everyone is gifted, everyone is diligent. These are simply the minimum skills. Far more important is an attitude of mind. Along the corridor I boast a colleague who in 1945 drafted a memorandum to the government advising them not to accept the Volkswagen works as war reparation, because the Volkswagen plainly had no commercial future. I must tell you, unlikely as it may seem, that man has risen to the very, very top. All

sorts of diplomatic virtues he displays. He has
forbearance. He is gracious. He is sociable. Perhaps you
begin to understand . . .

SUSAN: You are saying . . .

CHARLESON: I am saying that certain qualities are valued here
above a simple gift of being right or wrong. Qualities
sometimes hard to define . . .

SUSAN: What you are saying is that nobody may speak, nobody
may question . . .

CHARLESON: Certainly tact is valued very high.
(*Pause.* SUSAN *very low.*)

SUSAN: Sir Andrew, do you never find it in yourself to despise a
profession in which nobody may speak their mind?

CHARLESON: That is the nature of the service, Mrs Brock. It is
called diplomacy. And in its practice the English lead the
world. (*He smiles.*) The irony is this: we had an empire to
administer, there were six hundred of us in this place. Now
it's to be dismantled and there are six thousand. As our
power declines, the fight among us for access to that power
becomes a little more urgent, a little uglier perhaps. As our
influence wanes, as our empire collapses, there is little to
believe in. Behaviour is all.
(*Pause.*)
This is a lesson which you both must learn.
(*A moment, then* SUSAN *picks up her handbag to go.*)

SUSAN: I must thank you for your frankness, Sir Andrew . . .

CHARLESON: Not at all.

SUSAN: I must, however, warn you of my plan. If Brock is not
promoted in the next six days, I am intending to shoot myself.
(SUSAN *gets up from her seat.* CHARLESON *follows quickly.*)
Now thank you, and I shan't stay for the drink . . .

CHARLESON: (*Calls*) Begley . . .

SUSAN: I'm due at a reception for Australia Day.
(CHARLESON *moves quickly to the inner door.* SUSAN *begins talking
very fast as she moves to go.*)

CHARLESON: Begley.

SUSAN: I always like to see just how rude I can be. Not that the

Australians ever notice, of course. So it does become a
sort of Zen sport, don't you think?

(BEGLEY *appears*.)

CHARLESON: John, I wonder, could you give me a hand?

BEGLEY: Sir.

(SUSAN *stops near the door, starts talking yet more rapidly*.)

SUSAN: Ah the side-kick, the placid young man, now where have
I seen that character before?

CHARLESON: If we could take Mrs Brock down to the surgery . . .

SUSAN: I assure you, Sir Andrew, I'm perfectly all right.

CHARLESON: Perhaps alert her husband . . .

BEGLEY: If you're not feeling well . . .

SUSAN: People will be waiting at Australia House. I can't let
them down. It will be packed with angry people all
searching for me, saying where is she, what a let-down. I
only came here to be insulted and now there's no
chance.

(CHARLESON *looks at* BEGLEY *as if to co-ordinate a move. They
advance slightly*.)

CHARLESON: I think it would be better if you . . .

(SUSAN *starts to shout*.)

SUSAN: Please. Please leave me alone.

(CHARLESON *and* BEGLEY *stop*. SUSAN *is hysterical. She waits a
moment*.)

I can't . . . always manage with people.

(*Pause*.)

I think you have destroyed my husband, you see.

SCENE 10

Knightsbridge. Easter 1962.

*From the dark the sound of some stately orchestral chords: Mahler,
melodic, solemn. It is evening. The room has been restored to its former
rather old-fashioned splendour. The curtains are drawn. At a mahogany
table sits* ALICE. *She is putting a large pile of leaflets into brown*

envelopes. Very little disturbs the rhythm of her work. She is dressed
exactly as for Scene 1.

BROCK *is sitting at another table at the front of the stage. He has an*
abacus in front of him and a pile of ledgers and cheque stubs. He is
dressed in cavalry twills with a check shirt open at the neck.

The music stops. The stereo machine switches itself off.

BROCK: Well, I suppose it isn't too bad. Perhaps we'll keep going
another couple of years. A regime of mineral water and
lightly browned toast.
(*He smiles and stretches. Then turns to look at* ALICE. *There is a*
bottle of mineral water on the table in front of her.)
I assume she's still in there.

ALICE: She paces around.
(BROCK *gets up and pours some out.*)

BROCK: I told her this morning . . . we'll have to sell the house.
I'm sure we can cope in a smaller sort of flat. Especially
now we don't have to entertain.
(*He takes a sip.*)
I can't help feeling it will be better, I'm sure. Too much
money. I think that's what went wrong. Something about it
corrupts the will to live. Too many years spent sploshing
around.
(*He suddenly listens.*)
What?

ALICE: Nothing. She's just moving about.
(*He turns to* ALICE.)

BROCK: Perhaps you'd enjoy to take the evening off. I'm happy
to do duty for an hour or two.

ALICE: I enjoy it. I get to do my work. A good long slog for my
charity appeal. And I've rather fallen out with all those
people I knew. And most of them go off on the Aldermaston
March.

BROCK: Really? Of course. Easter weekend.
(*He picks his way through the remains of an Indian takeaway meal*
which is on ALICE's *table, searching for good scraps.*

ALICE: Except for Alistair and I've no intention of spending an

evening with him—or her, as he's taken to calling
himself.

BROCK: How come?

ALICE: Apparently he's just had his penis removed.

BROCK: Voluntarily? It's what he intended, I mean?

ALICE: I believe. In Morocco. And replaced with a sort of pink
plastic envelope. I haven't seen it. He says he keeps the
shopping list in there, tucks five pound notes away, so he
says.

BROCK: I thought that strange young girl of yours would ring.

(ALICE *looks up for a moment from her work.*)

ALICE: No, no. She decided to move on. There's some appalling
politician, I'm told. On the paedophiliac wing of the Tory
party. She's going to spend the summer swabbing the deck on
his yacht. Pleasuring his enormous underside. It's what she
always wanted. The fat. The inane.

(*She looks up again.*)

If you've nothing to do, you could give a hand with these.

(BROCK *takes no notice, casts aside the scraps.*)

BROCK: Looking back, I seem to have been eating all the time. My
years in the Foreign Service, I mean. I don't think I missed a
single canapé. Not one. The silver tray flashed and bang, I
was there.

ALICE: Do you miss it?

BROCK: Almost all the time. There's not much glamour in
insurance, you know.

(*He smiles.*)

Something in the Foreign Office suited my style. Whatever
horrible things people say. At least they were hypocrites, I do
value that now. Hypocrisy does keep things pleasant for at
least part of the time. Whereas down in the City they don't
even try.

ALICE: You chose it.

BROCK: That's right. That isn't so strange. The strange bit is
always . . . why I remain.

(*He stands staring a moment.*)

Still, it gives her something new to despise. The sad thing is this time . . . I despise it as well.

(ALICE *reaches for a typed list of names, pushes aside the pile of envelopes.*)

ALICE: Eight hundred addresses, eight hundred names . . .

(BROCK *turns and looks at her.*)

BROCK: You were never attracted? A regular job?

ALICE: I never had time. Too busy relating to various young
men. Falling in and out of love turns out to be like any
other career.

(*She looks up.*)

I had an idea that lust . . . that lust was very good. And
could be made simple. And cheering. And light. Perhaps I
was simply out of my time.

BROCK: You speak as if it's over.

ALICE: I've no doubt it is.

(*Pause.*)

BROCK: How long since anyone took a look next door?

ALICE: That's why I think it may be time to do good.

(SUSAN *opens the door, standing dressed as for Scene 1. She is a
little dusty.*)

SUSAN: I need to ask you to move out of here. I am in temporary
need of this room. You can go wherever you like. And
pretty soon also . . . you're welcome to return.

(*She goes off at once to the desk where she picks items off the surface
and throws them quietly into cubbyholes.* ALICE *is looking at*
BROCK.)

BROCK: You'd better tell me, Susan, what you've done to your
hands.

SUSAN: I've just been taking some paper from the wall.

BROCK: There's blood.

SUSAN: A fingernail.

(*Pause.*)

BROCK: Susan, what have you actually done?

(BROCK *gets up and goes to the door, looks down the corridor.* SUSAN
stands facing the desk, speaks quietly.)

SUSAN: I thought as we were going to get rid of the house . . .
and I couldn't stand any of the things that were there . . .

(*He turns back into the room. She turns and looks at him.*)
Now what's best to be doing in here?
(BROCK *looks at her, speaks as quietly.*)
BROCK: Could you look in the drawer please, Alice, there's some
Nembutal . . .
ALICE: I'm not sure we should . . .
BROCK: I shan't ask you again.
(ALICE *slides open the drawer, puts a small bottle of pills on the
table.* BROCK *moves a pace towards* SUSAN.)
Listen, if we're going to have to sell this house . . .
SUSAN: You yourself said it, I've often heard you say, it's money
that did it, it's money that rots. That we've all lived like
camels off the fat in our humps. Well, then, isn't the best
thing to do . . . to turn round simply and give the house
away?
(*She smiles.*)
Alice, would this place suit your needs? Somewhere to set
down all your unmarried mothers. If we lay out mattresses,
mattresses on the floor . . .
ALICE: Well, I . . .
SUSAN: Don't your women need a place to live?
(*Without warning she raises her arms above her head.*)
By our own hands.
Pause.)
Of our own free will. An Iranian vase. A small wooden Buddha.
Twelve marble birds copied from an Ottoman king.
(*Pause.*)
How can they be any possible use? Look out the bedroom
window, I've thrown them away.
(*She opens the door and goes at once into the corridor. At once* BROCK
crosses the room to the desk to look for his address book. ALICE *starts
clearing up the leaflets and envelopes on the table in front of her.*)
BROCK: I suppose you conspired.
ALICE: Not at all.
BROCK: Well, really?
ALICE: That was the first that I've heard.
BROCK: In that case, please, you might give me some help. Find

out what else she's been doing out there.

(SUSAN *reappears dragging in two packing cases, already half full. She then starts gathering objects from around the room.*)

SUSAN: Cutlery, crockery, lampshades and books, books, books. Encyclopaedias. Clutter. Meaningless. A universe of things.

(*She starts to throw them one by one into the crates.*)

Mosquito nets, golf clubs, photographs. China. Marble. Glass. Mementoes in stone. What is this shit? What are these godforsaken bloody awful things?

(BROCK *turns, still speaking quietly.*)

BROCK: Which is the braver? To live as I do? Or never, ever to face life like you?

(*He holds up the small card he has found.*)

This is the doctor's number, my dear. With my permission he can put you inside. I am quite capable of doing it tonight. So why don't you start to put all those things back?

(*A pause.* SUSAN *looks at him, then to* ALICE.)

SUSAN: Alice, would your women value my clothes?

ALICE: Well, I . . .

SUSAN: It sounds fairly silly. I have thirteen evening dresses, though.

BROCK: Susan.

SUSAN: Obviously not much use as they are. But possibly they could be re-cut. Re-sewn?

(*She reaches out and with one hand picks up an ornament from the mantelpiece which she throws with a crash into the crate. A pause.*)

BROCK: Your life is selfish, self-interested gain. That's the most charitable interpretation to hand. You claim to be protecting some personal ideal, always at a cost of almost infinite pain to everyone around you. You are selfish, brutish, unkind. Jealous of other people's happiness as well, determined to destroy other ways of happiness they find. I've spent fifteen years of my life trying to help you, simply trying to be kind, and my great comfort has been that I am waiting for some indication from you . . . some sign that you have valued this kindness of mine. Some love perhaps. Insane.

(*He smiles.*)

And yet . . . I really shan't ever give up, I won't surrender till you're well again. And that to me would mean your admitting one thing: that in the life you have led you have utterly failed, failed in the very, very heart of your life. Admit it. Then perhaps you might really move on.

(*Pause.*)

Now I'm going to go and give our doctor a ring. I plan at last to beat you at your own kind of game. I am going to play as dirtily and ruthlessly as you. And this time I am certainly not giving in.

(BROCK *goes out. A pause.*)

SUSAN: Well.

(*Pause.*)

Well, goodness. What's best to do?

(*Pause.*)

What's the best way to start stripping this room?

(SUSAN *doesn't move.* ALICE *stands watching.*)

ALICE: Susan, I think you should get out of this house.

SUSAN: Of course.

ALICE: I'll help you. Any way I can.

SUSAN: Well, that's very kind.

ALICE: If you . . .

SUSAN: I'll be going just as soon as this job is done.

(*Pause.*)

ALICE: Listen, if Raymond really means what he says . . .

(SUSAN *turns and looks straight at* ALICE.)

You haven't even asked me, Susan, you see. You haven't asked me yet what I think of the idea.

(SUSAN *frowns.*)

SUSAN: Really, Alice, I shouldn't need to ask. It's a very sad day when one can't help the poor.

(ALICE *suddenly starts to laugh.* SUSAN *sets off across the room, resuming a completely normal social manner.*)

ALICE: For God's sake, Susan, he'll put you in the bin.

SUSAN: Don't be silly, Alice, it's Easter weekend. It must have occurred to you . . . the doctor's away.

(BROCK *reappears at the open door, the address book in his hand.* SUSAN *turns to him.*)

All right, Raymond? Anything I can do? I've managed to rout out some whisky over here.

(*She sets the bottle down on the table, next to the Nembutal.*)

Alice was just saying she might slip out for a while. Give us a chance to sort our problems out. I'm sure if we had a really serious talk . . . I could keep going till morning. Couldn't you?

(SUSAN *turns to* ALICE.)

All right, Alice?

ALICE: Yes. Yes, of course. I'm going, I'm just on my way.

(*She picks up her coat and heads for the door.*)

All right if I get back in an hour or two? I don't like to feel I'm intruding. You know?

(*She smiles at* SUSAN. *Then closes the door.* SUSAN *at once goes back to the table.* BROCK *stands watching her.*)

SUSAN: Now, Raymond. Good. Let's look at this thing.

(SUSAN *pours out a spectacularly large scotch, filling the glass to the very rim. Then she pushes it a few inches across the table to* BROCK.)

Where would be the best place to begin?

SCENE 11

Blackpool. June 1962.
  From the dark music. Then silence. Two voices in the dark.

LAZAR: Susan. Susan. Feel who I am.

SUSAN: I know. I know who you are. How could you be anyone else but Lazar?

(*And a small bedside light comes on.* LAZAR *and* SUSAN *are lying sideways across a double bed, facing opposite ways. They are in a sparsely furnished and decaying room.* LAZAR *is in his coat, facing away from us as he reaches for the nightlight.* SUSAN *is also fully dressed, in a big black man's overcoat, her hair wild, her dress crumpled round her thighs. The bedside light barely illuminates them at all.*)

Jesus. Jesus. To be happy again.

(*At once* SUSAN *gets up and goes into what must be the bathroom. A shaft of yellow light from the doorway falls across the bed.*)

LAZAR: Don't take your clothes off whatever you do.

SUSAN: (*Off*) Of course not.

LAZAR: That would spoil it hopelessly for me.

SUSAN: (*Off*) I'm getting my cigarettes. I roll my own . . .

LAZAR: Goodness me.

SUSAN: Tell you, there are no fucking flies on me.

(*She has reappeared with her holdall which is crumpled and stained. She sits cross-legged on the end of the bed. She starts to roll two cigarettes.*)

LAZAR: I am glad I found you.

SUSAN: I'm just glad I came.

LAZAR: This place is filthy.

SUSAN: It's a cheap hotel.

LAZAR: They seem to serve you dust on almost everything.

SUSAN: You should be grateful for dust, did you know? If it weren't for all the dust in the atmosphere, human beings would be killed by the heat of the sun.

LAZAR: In Blackpool?

SUSAN: Well . . .

LAZAR: Are you kidding me?

(SUSAN *reaches into the overcoat pocket.*)

SUSAN: I was given some grass. Shall I roll it in?

LAZAR: Just the simple cigarette for me.

(SUSAN *nods.*)

I hope you didn't mind my choosing Blackpool at all. It's just that I work near . . .

SUSAN: Don't tell me any more.

LAZAR: Susan . . .

(*Pause.*)

Will you . . . can you touch me again?

(SUSAN *facing away doesn't move, just smiles. A pause.*)

Do you know how I found you? Through the BBC. I just

caught that programme a few months ago. They told
me you were married and based in London now. They gave
me an address . . .

SUSAN: I left it weeks ago.

LAZAR: I know. I gather you've been out on the road. But . . . I
went, I went round and saw the man . . .

SUSAN: And how was he?

LAZAR: He looked like a man who'd spent his life with you.

SUSAN: How can you say that?

LAZAR: (*Smiles*) Oh I'm guessing, that's all.
  (SUSAN *smiles again.*)
  He said he'd only just managed to reclaim.

SUSAN: Oh really? That's my fault. I gave the house away.

LAZAR: He said he'd had to fight to get back into his home.
  There'd been some kind of trouble. Police, violence it
  seems . . .

SUSAN: Was he angry?

LAZAR: Angry? No. He just seemed very sorry not to be with
  you.
  (*Pause.* SUSAN *stops rolling the cigarette.*)

SUSAN: Listen, I have to tell you I've not always been well. I
  have a weakness. I like to lose control. I've been letting it
  happen, well, a number of times . . .

LAZAR: Is it . . .

SUSAN: I did shoot someone about ten years ago.

LAZAR: Did you hurt him?

SUSAN: Fortunately no. At least that's what we kept telling him,
  you know. Raymond went and gave him money in notes.
  He slapped them like hot poultices all over his wounds. I
  think it did finally convince him on the whole. It was after
  Raymond's kindness I felt I had to get engaged . . .

LAZAR: Why do people . . .

SUSAN: Marry? I don't know. Are you . . . ?
  (*Pause.*)

LAZAR: What? Ask me anything at all.

SUSAN: No. It's nothing. I don't want to know. (*She smiles again.*)

LAZAR: Do you ever see him?

SUSAN: Good gracious no. I've stripped away everything,
everything I've known. There's only one kind of dignity,
that's in living alone. The clothes you stand up in, the
world you can see . . .

LAZAR: Oh Susan . . .

SUSAN: Don't.

(*Pause.* SUSAN *is suddenly still.*)

I want to believe in you. So tell me nothing. That's best.

(*Pause.* SUSAN *does not turn round.* LAZAR *suddenly gets up, and
goes to get his coat and gloves from his suitcase.* SUSAN *looks down
at the unmade cigarette in her hands. Then she starts to make the
roll-up again.*)

SUSAN: How long till dawn? Do you think we should go? If we
wait till morning we'll have to pay the bill. I can't believe
that can be the right thing to do.

(*She smiles.*)

Is there an early train, do you know? Though just where
I'm going I'm not really sure. There aren't many people
who'll have me, you know.

(*Pause.*)

I hope you'll forgive me. The grass has gone in.

(*She licks along the edge of the joint, then lights it.* LAZAR *stands
still, his suitcase beside him.*)

LAZAR: I don't know what I'd expected.

SUSAN: Mmm?

LAZAR: What I'd hoped for, at the time I returned. Some sort of
edge to the life that I lead. Some sort of feeling their death
was worthwhile.

(*Pause.*)

Some day I must tell you. I don't feel I've done well. I gave
in. Always. All along the line. Suburb. Wife. Hell. I work in
a corporate bureaucracy as well . . .

(SUSAN *has begun to giggle*)

SUSAN: Lazar, I'm sorry, I'm just about to go.

LAZAR: What?

SUSAN: I've eaten nothing. So I just go . . .

(*She waves vaguely with her hand. Then smiles. A pause.*)

LAZAR: I hate, I hate this life that we lead.

SUSAN: Oh God, here I go.

(*Pause.*)

Kiss me. Kiss me now as I go.

(LAZAR *moves towards* SUSAN *and tries to take her in his arms. But as he tries to kiss her, she falls back on to the bed, flopping down where she stays.*

LAZAR *removes the roach from her hand. Puts it out. Goes over and closes his case. Then picks it up. Goes to the bathroom and turns the light off. Now only the nightlight is on.* LAZAR *goes to the door.*)

LAZAR: A fine undercover agent will move so that nobody can ever tell he was there.

(LAZAR *turns the nightlight off. Darkness.*)

SUSAN: Tell me your name.

(*Pause.*)

LAZAR: Code name.

(*Pause.*)

Code name.

(*Pause.*)

Code name Lazar.

(LAZAR *opens the door of the room. At once music plays. Where you would expect a corridor you see the fields of France shining brilliantly in a fierce green square. The room scatters.*)

SCENE 12

St Benoît, August 1944.

The darkened areas of the room disappear and we see a French hillside in high summer. The stage picture forms piece by piece. Green, yellow, brown. Trees. The fields stretch away. A high sun. A brilliant August day. Another FRENCHMAN *stands looking down into the valley. He carries a spade, is in wellingtons and corduroys. He is about 40, fattish with an unnaturally gloomy air.*

Then SUSAN *appears climbing the hill. She is 19. She is dressed like a young French girl, her pullover over her shoulder. She looks radiantly well.*

FRENCHMAN: Bonjour, ma'moiselle.

SUSAN: Bonjour.

FRENCHMAN: Vous regardez le village?

SUSAN: Oui, je suis montée la colline pour mieux voir. C'est merveilleux.

FRENCHMAN: Oui. Indeed the day is fine.

(*Pause.* SUSAN *looks across at the* FRENCHMAN.)

FRENCHMAN: We understand. We know. The war is over now.

SUSAN: 'I climbed the hill to get a better view.' (*She smiles.*) I've only spoken French for months on end.

FRENCHMAN: You are English?

(SUSAN *nods.*)

Tower Bridge.

SUSAN: Just so.

(*The* FRENCHMAN *smiles and walks over to join* SUSAN. *Together they look away down the hill.*)

FRENCHMAN: You join the party in the village?

SUSAN: Soon. I'm hoping, yes, I'm very keen to go.

FRENCHMAN: Myself I work. A farmer. Like any other day. The Frenchman works or starves. He is the piss. The shit. The lowest of the low.

(SUSAN *moves forward a little, staring down the hill.*)

SUSAN: Look. They're lighting fires in the square. And children . . . coming out with burning sticks.

(*Pause.*)

Have you seen anything as beautiful as this?

(SUSAN *stands looking out. The* FRENCHMAN *mumbles ill-humouredly.*)

FRENCHMAN: The harvest is not good again this year.

SUSAN: I'm sorry.

(*The* FRENCHMAN *shrugs.*)

FRENCHMAN: As I expect. The land is very poor. I have to work each moment of the day.

SUSAN: But you'll be glad I think. You're glad as well?

(SUSAN *turns, so the* FRENCHMAN *cannot avoid the question. He reluctantly concedes.*)

FRENCHMAN: I'm glad. Is something good, is true. (*He looks puzzled.*) The English . . . have no feelings, yes? Are stiff.

SUSAN: They hide them, hide them from the world.

FRENCHMAN: Is stupid.

SUSAN: Stupid, yes. It may be . . .

(*Pause.*)

FRENCHMAN: Huh?

SUSAN: That things will quickly change. We have grown up. We will improve our world.

(*The* FRENCHMAN *stares at* SUSAN. *Then offers gravely:*)

FRENCHMAN: Perhaps . . . perhaps you like some soup. My wife.

SUSAN: All right.

(SUSAN *smiles. They look at each other, about to go.*)

FRENCHMAN: The walk is down the hill.

SUSAN: My friend.

(*Pause.*)

There will be days and days and days like this.